QUICK & EASY VEGETARIAN COOKBOOK

Quick & Easy

Vegetarian Cookbook

75 Recipes for Satisfying Meatless Meals

ANNA-MARIE WALSH

ROCKRIDGE
PRESS

For general information on our other products and services or to obtain technical support, please contact our Customer Care Department within the United States at (866) 744-2665, or outside the United States at (510) 253-0500.

Rockridge Press publishes its books in a variety of electronic and print formats. Some content that appears in print may not be available in electronic books, and vice versa.

TRADEMARKS: Rockridge Press and the Rockridge Press logo are trademarks or registered trademarks of Callisto Media Inc. and/or its affiliates, in the United States and other countries, and may not be used without written permission. All other trademarks are the property of their respective owners. Rockridge Press is not associated with any product or vendor mentioned in this book.

Interior and Cover Designer: Sean Doyle
Art Producer: Tom Hood
Editor: Cecily McAndrews
Production Editor: Jenna Dutton
Production Manager: Martin Worthington

Photography © Annie Martin, cover and p. vi; Jennifer Davick, p. ii; Andrew Urwin/Stocksy, p. x; Magdalena Hendey/Stockfood, p. 14; Ina Peters/Stocksy, p. 28; Tatjana Zlatkovic/Stocksy, p. 40; Gareth Morgans/Stockfood, p. 62; Ivan Solis/Stocksy, p. 84; Bauer Syndication/Stockfood, p. 102; Andrew Purcell, p. 114.

Cover: Avocado and Lemon Pasta, p. 88

Paperback ISBN: 978-1-64876-752-4
eBook ISBN: 978-1-64876-753-1

R0

To my MOM, *who inspires me every day. To* STEVE, *who will always be my rock. To* SHARON, *who taught me faith and forgiveness is everything. And to my* DAD, *who taught me never to give up.*

Contents

Introduction

〉〉 〈〈

started my vegetarian journey in 2010 after visiting my parents in New York City. I had dinner at the Hard Rock Cafe with my stepfather, Steve, and we ordered nachos, one of my favorite dishes. Only my stepfather had recently stopped eating dairy and meat. So, when the nachos came to the table, it was basically just tortilla chips and salsa. No cheese, no sour cream . . . no fun. Despite this seemingly unpromising start, I was surprised at how easy it was to forego meat and still eat delicious meals. Strangely, I was inspired.

When I returned home to Orlando, I began to explore vegetarianism. As time went on, my sleep improved, my energy levels went way up, and in general, I just felt better. I was also being more creative in the kitchen and enjoying a whole new world of vegetables and grains.

While I was embarking on this new way of eating, I decided to start a blog recording my newfound love of vegetable dishes. *Beauty and the Beets* was a way for me to document what I was eating and preparing in my home kitchen. In the beginning, the only visitors I had to my blog were those who shared my last name (Hi, Mom and Dad!). But then, a few years later, I published a copycat version of the Kale Peanut Salad at Houston's Restaurant (it's so, so good), and suddenly, more people were coming to my blog and sending me messages about how much they loved my stories and recipes. Eventually, cooking and writing about food became my full-time job.

I have since enrolled in several nutrition classes so that I could officially learn more about food and the positive effects of a healthy diet. Don't get me wrong, boxed mac and cheese is still my all-time favorite comfort food, and I will stray from the veg path and eat a tuna steak every now and then, but the basis of my diet revolves around eating vegetables, whole grains, beans, and legumes.

My goal in writing this book is not only to make it look (and feel) easy, but also to convince you that eating vegetarian can be simple and tasty. Whether you are a carnivore hoping to incorporate more vegetables into your diet, or a flexitarian, pescatarian, vegetarian, vegan, or something in between, I hope you find these recipes fun, easy to make, and flavorful. I hope it inspires you to think a bit outside the box when it comes to using produce in your everyday cooking.

Egg and Avocado Toast, page 26

CHAPTER ONE

Vegetarian Made Easy and Fast

❖

Vegetarian cooking doesn't mean doubling up on side dishes and calling it a meal. Vegetables are quite capable of taking center stage as entrées all on their own. With the right recipes and techniques, vegetarian cooking is also quick and easy. You might even call it fun. And, most important, delicious.

The Wonders of Vegetarian Cooking

Some people think vegetarian cooking is boring or sad. These people don't understand the versatility of cauliflower or how delicious a perfect butternut squash "steak" can be, and that's okay. You'll soon see that Brussels sprouts are the greatest vegetable in the world (maybe this is a personal opinion) or that a fast-food taco can't compete with vegetarian Double Decker Broccoli Tacos (page 74). Plus, a veggie burger (like the Carrot and White-Bean Veggie Burger, page 78) can be just as satisfying and delicious as its meaty counterpart. You can eat them more often *and* still feel great after.

HEARTY FOOD

The beauty of vegetables is that they can transform into so many different dishes. Cauliflower and walnuts can become meaty crumbles easily thrown into pasta dishes, salads, or tacos. Avocado makes a super creamy pasta sauce. Portobello mushrooms make a great Philly cheesesteak. Vegetables are quite versatile and can be enjoyed the same ways as meat and very often cooked the same as well. Eating vegetarian doesn't mean boring. As a matter of fact, it's quite the opposite! Different vegetables add different colors, textures, and tastes to any dish.

Many people question whether vegetarians have enough protein in their diets. But there are so many options for protein. Although some vegetables have more protein than others (think green peas, spinach, broccoli, and edamame), there are plenty of other ways vegetarians can get their fill. Beans, seeds, and nuts pack a protein-filled punch and are easy additions to most dishes. Beans, ever versatile, make a great addition to soups, salads, and casseroles. Chia seeds, sesame seeds, and flaxseed can be added to just about any dish without drastically affecting the flavor profile. As you cook more vegetarian meals, you will quickly learn how to combine proteins and fats with vegetables, and you will be surprised how easy it is to create satisfying, hearty meals.

DIETARY OPTIONS

Throughout the book, you will find easy, straightforward recipes that work for all sorts of diets, including vegans and people with allergies. Cheese and other dairy ingredients are probably the easiest ingredients to eliminate to make a

COOKING FOR FLEX HOUSEHOLDS

Here's a common situation: Maybe you have one child who has decided to become a full vegan, your spouse refuses to give up meat, and someone else in your house follows a strict gluten-free diet. Such is life; different people have different needs, but this can make dinner frustrating. Luckily, many of these easy dishes can accommodate different palates and needs. For instance, you could easily serve some sautéed fish with the Orange and Edamame Salad with Carrot Vinaigrette (page 57), or swap in gluten-free pasta in the Avocado and Lemon Pasta (page 88). I've found that using a gluten-free pasta or flour in place of its gluten counterpart rarely affects the flavor of a dish.

dish vegan. I only drink nut milks and I have never run into a recipe where the flavor or texture was affected by swapping dairy milk for nondairy milk. I have offered tips to change things up where appropriate, but you can also make your own substitutions by taking advantage of the various dairy-free cheese, yogurt, and vegan mayonnaise options you can find at the grocery store. Just keep in mind that these dairy-free options aren't always healthier than their dairy counterparts. Read the labels for sugar, sodium, and fat content.

VARIETY

The recipes in this book use a wide variety of vegetables, and I've made swapping suggestions in the recipes as well (I get it, not everyone likes mushrooms). Different vegetables and cooking techniques create different flavors and textures, so you will not feel like you are eating the same thing over and over. Starches are so easy to swap out: Cooked rice, quinoa, farro, and couscous are mostly interchangeable, and, unless otherwise noted, can easily sub in for each other in most recipes. You will find that I do not buy soy crumbles, or those meaty alternatives found in the freezer section of grocery stores. I like to make my own crumbles and meat substitutes with vegetables and legumes. It's exciting to me how much you can make with a few simple vegetables and a grain, and I hope it will become exciting to you, too.

Cooking Strategies

As I stated earlier, vegetarian cooking doesn't have to be daunting or laborious. It also doesn't have to be a collection of bland side dishes. Throughout the book, I've employed a few strategies to streamline cooking time and still craft some amazing dishes. All the recipes in this book fall into at least one of the following categories, and are labeled as such, so you can decide exactly what type of quick and easy you're in the mood for today.

QUICK

Time is money, and we always want more of both, which is why you will find a number of recipes in the book with a "Quick" label on them. These dishes can be prepared from start to finish in 30 minutes or less. That's right. Prepping the ingredients, cooking, and plating will be done in less time than it takes to watch the evening news. I have also included some tips on prepping ingredients to save even more time in the kitchen. And of course, you can always buy your vegetables already diced or sliced. Though pre-cleaned and chopped veggies are a bit more expensive than buying whole vegetables, sometimes the time you save is worth the extra money. Buy pre-diced onions and peppers, and the One-Pot Rice and Bean Casserole (page 70) will come together in no time at all.

5-INGREDIENT

Yes, it is possible to create a meal using minimal ingredients while maximizing flavor. Recipes labeled "5-Ingredient" contain five ingredients or less (not counting salt, pepper, and oil, as these are simple staples in most kitchens). These dishes are usually the easiest to throw together and perfect for anyone who lives in a small space with minimal storage. For example, my Chickpea and Avocado Mash Sandwiches (page 43) contain only four ingredients (including the bread), but it is one of my favorite simple lunches.

ONE POT

Dishes with this label save time because you won't spend hours *after* your meal scrubbing the dishes. And by "One Pot," I actually mean "one dish," as the recipe might be made in a stockpot, baking dish, or sheet pan. Many pasta dishes, soups, and casseroles have this label, like my Eggplant Parmesan Bake (page 76) or the Baked Cheesy Zucchini Boats on (page 65). Refer to the equipment list section of this book to learn about size specifications and materials of these pots, casserole dishes, and sheet pans.

NO COOK

Cook time: zero; flavor factor: infinite. Sometimes you just don't want to turn on the oven and heat up the kitchen. Recipes labeled "No Cook" mean just that. They entail no cooking, baking, sautéing, boiling, or roasting. And no microwaves, either. Salads are obvious candidates, but you'd be surprised at how many other things you can whip up without the heat. And we're not talking raw diet. It's okay to buy eggs already hard-boiled at the grocery store or add pre-cooked zucchini noodles. It's not cheating; it's being smart about your time and energy.

OFF THE SHELF

This label simply means that these recipes use ingredients that are almost entirely from ingredients you most likely already have in your pantry or freezer, with the addition of some basic items like milk, eggs, or bread. In other words, the recipes call for shelf-stable items or long-lasting or frozen produce, so you can reach into the back of your pantry or freezer and come up with a meal. These recipes are great for using up what I call "lost and found" items, like the can of beans I didn't know I had until I (re-)found them in my pantry. There are several recipes in this book that call for frozen vegetables, such as the Tarragon-Marinated Brussels Sprouts (page 32) or the Chilled Pea and Mint Soup (page 50). It's always good to keep an inventory of what you have waiting for you in your pantry or freezer, so you use them before the expiration date or before the impending doom of freezer burn.

KITCHEN SHORTCUTS

I am all about streamlining my cooking to save time. While you are more than welcome to soak and cook your own dried beans (it is a money saver), all the recipes in this book use canned beans. I am also a big fan of buying boxed vegetable stock, jarred marinara sauce, and pre-cut vegetables when the need arises. Store-bought hummus will save you a lot of time (and dirty dishes) for use in the Double Decker Broccoli Tacos (page 74). (Not to mention that, for this same recipe, you can also buy riced broccoli if your grocery store sells it.) And never underestimate the time-saving power of a microwave. Potatoes cook so much faster in a microwave than in an oven and taste just as good. I am also a big fan of gadgets. I use an egg cooker in the microwave to hard boil eggs faster than boiling them on the stove. Frozen veggies are a twofold time-saver because they save time in the prepping and the cooking process.

Planning meals ahead of time also saves time. For example, you could make a double batch of the Cauliflower and Walnut "Meat" Crumbles (page 64). Then, later in the week, add the leftover crumbles to the One-Pot Vegan Mac and Cheese (page 97) or the Vegetarian Taco Salad (page 60). Double the recipe of the Vegan Blue-Cheese Dressing (page 46) for the Buffalo Chickpea Pita Sandwiches (page 46) and use it later in the week to top the Vegetarian Niçoise Salad (page 53).

The Efficient Vegetarian Kitchen

Smart meal planning requires having a kitchen that is maximized for quick and easy vegetarian cooking, including the right ingredient staples, tools, and equipment.

THE STAPLES

I like to stock up on basics, especially when they go on sale (did you know the average sale cycle of most products at major grocery stores is six weeks?). This way, whether I am whipping up something fancy or making a basic Off the Shelf dish, I never need to go to the neighbor and ask for an egg. I keep a small magnetic whiteboard on my refrigerator so as I use the last of a basic staple item, I can just add it to the list instead of going through my pantry or freezer every time I need to create a grocery list. Salt, pepper, and olive oil are forever staples in my kitchen. All the items listed here will be used in the recipes in the book several times, so having them at the ready will make your dinner hour so much easier.

Fresh Ingredients

Carrots. Carrots are so underrated. Not only can you eat them raw, but they can be turned into fries, veggie burgers, slaw dogs, and vinaigrette.

Cauliflower. Cauliflower is another vegetable that can be used in many ways. Riced, boiled, roasted, and sautéed, cauliflower is super versatile.

Garlic. Garlic is always good to have on hand because it will add flavor and heat to any dish. Although I do like to use minced garlic in a jar, I will add fresh garlic to summer pastas and salad dressing.

Potatoes. A baked potato can be a meal, but potatoes can also be mashed, shredded, or roasted to add a little starch to any meal. I especially like to have a couple of baking potatoes on hand for dinner in a pinch.

Tomatoes. Tomatoes are a perfect addition to salads, pastas, tacos, and rice bowls. They can be chopped, minced, sliced, and diced; whatever the recipe calls for, tomatoes can do.

Refrigerator and Freezer Ingredients

Eggs. Eggs are a basic protein for most diets. They make a quick breakfast, and can be used for flavor, moisture, and as a binding agent in a variety of dishes, from veggie burgers to desserts.

Firm Tofu. Tofu is the chameleon of proteins. It takes on the flavor of whatever sauce you cook it in, and can, for example, mimic the blue cheese crumbles in a Vegan Blue-Cheese Dressing (page 46).

Frozen Broccoli. Frozen broccoli is a perfect staple because it's already chopped, it lasts for a long time, and the freezing process retains the nutrients. Microwave-steamed broccoli can be added to soups, tacos, or pastas in a flash.

Frozen Chopped Onions. Don't feel like a good cry? These onions are already chopped for you. All you do is thaw them in a saucepan or in the microwave and they're ready for any dish.

Milk. Whether you prefer dairy or nondairy, milk is a versatile ingredient that can be used in soups and pasta dishes. Anytime I have a recipe that calls for milk, I use almond milk. Feel free to choose your own favorite, whether it be oat, cashew, soy, or plain old dairy milk.

Shredded Cheese. Shredded cheese is another great source of protein for vegetarians and can be mixed into sauces or be used as a topping or garnish for salads, soups, and pastas. I always like to keep shredded Parmesan and mozzarella cheeses on hand.

Pantry Ingredients

Black Pepper. Freshly ground black pepper is my preference for a fresher flavor, but pre-ground pepper will work as well. You can find small bottles of peppercorns with the grinder built right into the package in the spice aisle of the grocery store.

Canned Beans. I like to stock up on canned chickpeas, black beans, and red beans for adding protein to a variety of dishes. Chickpeas are, in my opinion, one of the most versatile ingredients used in vegetarian cooking, which is why they pop up all over this book.

Cooked Lentils. Buy lentils already cooked to save lots of time. They sometimes can be found in cans with the beans but other times are in pouches in the international aisle of most grocery stores.

Everything-Bagel Seasoning. Also referred to as EBS, this blend of sesame seeds, poppy seeds, sea salt, garlic, and onion flakes has made a splash in the last few years and can be used on anything and everything from roasted vegetables to scrambled eggs and cheese crisps.

Extra-Virgin Olive Oil. Extra-virgin olive oil (EVOO) is made from cold-pressed olives, whereas regular olive oil is a combination of cold-pressed and processed oils. Extra-virgin olive oil has a lovely, mild flavor, and it stands up to heat very well.

Jarred Marinara Sauce. I always look for marinara sauce without added sugar, as there can be a surprising amount of the stuff in store-bought, jarred sauces.

Minced Garlic. Although you can buy fresh garlic and chop it yourself, I always have a jar of minced garlic on hand. It saves so much time and, best of all, your hands won't smell like garlic for days.

Nut Butter. Beyond just spreading them on toast, nut butters like almond and cashew are great, nutritious ingredients. Use it in the peanut butter and jelly version of the Chocolate and Strawberry Puff Tarts (page 24) or Almond-Butter Oatmeal Energy Bites (page 33). Sunflower butter makes a great substitute for those with a nut allergy, because nut butters are fairly interchangeable.

Nutritional Yeast. This will be another go-to seasoning for just about every-thing, just like EBS. It adds a nutty and cheesy flavor, and it's my favorite way to season popcorn. It makes a great vegan substitute for Parmesan cheese.

Sea Salt. Sea salt works for most of the recipes in this book unless otherwise specified.

Vegetable Stock or Broth. In addition to using it for soups, broth works perfectly to cook rice or boil potatoes, just to give them a flavor boost. Vegetable stock adds a tangy, briny flavor that's hard to duplicate.

Vinegar. If I could keep only three vinegars in my pantry, I would have red wine, apple cider, and (wild card) tarragon vinegars: Red wine vinegar for basic vinaigrette, apple cider to make One-Pot Vegan Mac and Cheese (page 97) and pickled radishes, and tarragon to make fancier salad vinaigrettes to impress the guests.

TOOLS AND EQUIPMENT

Using the right tools and equipment can save you loads of time and energy when preparing meals. I would much rather shred Brussels sprouts in a food processor than shred them by hand. I am saving a bunch of time and saving my fingers from getting nicked. Although some tools are gimmicky, others are essential to running an efficient kitchen.

Essential Items

The recipes in this book do not require you to own special equipment like air-fryers or rice cookers, but there are some basic tools you need to have. This list is not exhaustive, but it's a good place to start.

- Baking pans: Large, rimmed sheet pans, a 9-by-13-inch baking dish
- Electric gadgets: 10-cup food processor, blender (a high-powered one is great, if you can afford it)
- Fire extinguisher
- Handheld gadgets: Potato masher, lemon juicer, citrus zester, kitchen scissors, can opener
- Large colander
- Measuring tools: a liquid measuring cup, plus measuring spoons and dry measuring cups
- Mixing bowls in a variety of sizes
- Parchment paper
- Pots and pans: 6-quart stockpot, large saucepot with a tight-fitting lid, large sauté pan with a high lip
- Utensils: Set of chef's knives, large ladle, wooden spoons, spatula, whisk, tongs

Nice-to-Have Items

These aren't necessary, but they will make your cooking experience more pleasant.

- Herb scissors
- Immersion blender
- Mason jars with tight lids
- Microwave egg cooker
- Pasta ladle

- Small mesh strainer
- Small rubber spatula
- Soup spoons
- Spoon rest

About the Recipes

We all lead busy lives, which is why I've developed these recipes with the busy person in mind. I've included additional time-saving tips wherever possible, and each recipe is labeled to accommodate various dietary restrictions and strategies. For instance, if you are short on time and want to cook with a minimum number of ingredients, try the Avocado and Lemon Pasta (page 88). Too tired to clean up after cooking? Make One-Pot Vegan Jambalaya (page 75).

LABELS

Some of the various labels you will find attached to the recipes in the book include:

5-Ingredient. Besides salt, pepper, and oil, these recipes require five ingredients or less.

Dairy-Free. No dairy is used in these recipes.

Gluten-Free. These recipes contain no gluten of any kind.

No Cook. No oven, stove, or microwave is needed to make any of these recipes.

Nut-Free. No nuts are used in the recipe.

Off the Shelf. These recipes are made with staples from the pantry or the freezer, with the addition of a few, very common fresh ingredients.

One Pot. Everything in these recipes can be made either in one pot, one dish, or on one sheet pan.

Quick. From start to finish, these recipes can be made in 30 minutes or less.

Vegan. A few recipes in the book are vegan without accommodations; many more are vegan with a few adjustments (in those cases, look for the Make it Vegan tip).

TIPS

Most recipes will offer some type of a tip to help you with the preparation of the dish. Here's a guide to the tips.

Ingredient Tip. These tips offer more information on selecting and buying ingredients, how to use them, and interesting nutrition facts.

Make it Vegan. Anytime a recipe can be made vegan, I add a tip to the recipe.

Quick Tip. These tips can aid you with faster preparation, cooking, or cleanup.

Variation Tip. Most recipes in this book can be changed easily by swapping in different vegetables or using a different spice to change the dish either a little or entirely.

Fresh Blueberry, Cream Cheese, and Cinnamon Rolls, page 19

CHAPTER TWO

Breakfast and Brunch

◇

CASHEW-CRUSTED FRENCH TOAST

PREP TIME: **10 MINUTES, PLUS 20 MINUTES REFRIGERATION**
COOK TIME: **10 MINUTES PER BATCH**

DAIRY-FREE, OFF THE SHELF, VEGAN

SERVES 4

2 cups raw unsalted cashews

2 cups water

½ teaspoon ground nutmeg

¼ teaspoon ground cinnamon

½ teaspoon pure vanilla extract

8 slices whole-wheat or whole-grain bread

Olive oil spray

Maple syrup, warmed, for serving

QUICK TIP: *This dish can be prepped up to step 3 the night before and left in the refrigerator overnight. In the morning, heat up the skillet and cook for a quick and easy breakfast.*

INGREDIENT TIP: *Raw unsalted cashews can be found in the bulk food aisle at most grocery stores.*

This cashew French toast is one of my favorite simple-yet-hearty breakfast dishes. The cashews not only add crunch and a heaping serving of heart-healthy fats and fiber, but they also provide protein to give you energy and sustain you until lunch. Top the French toast with warm maple syrup or add a dollop of whipped cream or strawberry puree (see Strawberry-Lemonade Ice Pops, page 106).

1. In a food processor, combine the cashews, water, nutmeg, cinnamon, and vanilla, and process until slightly chunky. Pour the mixture into a shallow dish.

2. Dip both sides of each slice of bread into the cashew mixture. In a shallow baking dish, place each dipped slice of bread in a single layer.

3. Pour any remaining cashew mixture over the bread, and cool in the refrigerator for 20 minutes.

4. Heat a large skillet over medium-high heat. Spray each side of the bread with olive oil spray, and put it in the skillet (you will most likely have to work in batches). Cook each side 4 to 5 minutes, or until golden brown. Transfer to a plate and keep warm. Repeat the process until all the bread has been cooked.

5. Drizzle the French toast with the warm maple syrup and serve.

VEGETABLE PIZZA FRITTATA

PREP TIME: 5 MINUTES   **COOK TIME: 25 MINUTES**

5-INGREDIENT, GLUTEN-FREE, NUT-FREE

SERVES 6

1 tablespoon olive oil, plus more for greasing

4 cups chopped vegetables, either one type or a mix (I like a mixture of mushrooms, onions, and peppers)

10 large eggs

3 tablespoons heavy cream

½ teaspoon salt

Freshly ground black pepper

1 cup shredded mozzarella cheese, divided

1 cup pizza sauce or marinara sauce, for drizzling

I love eating pizza for breakfast. But why not add pizza toppings to eggs and enjoy something a little more substantial than a cold slice of last night's takeout? I like using a combination of common pizza vegetables (such as mushrooms, onions, and peppers), but you can add any pizza topping of your choice. Pineapple and eggs? Sure, why not? Your pizza, your breakfast.

1. Preheat the oven to 400°F. Lightly grease a 9-by-13-inch baking dish with olive oil. Set it aside.

2. In a large skillet, heat 1 tablespoon of olive oil over medium heat. Add the chopped vegetables and cook until softened, stirring occasionally, about 10 minutes. Remove the pan from the heat.

3. In a medium mixing bowl, combine the eggs, heavy cream, salt, and pepper to taste, and whisk to mix well. Fold in half of the shredded cheese.

4. Spread the cooked vegetables in the prepared baking dish and pour the egg mixture over the vegetables.

5. Drizzle the pizza or marinara sauce over the top of the dish.

6. Sprinkle the remaining cheese on top of the casserole and bake for 20 minutes, until the cheese is golden and bubbly.

7. Remove the baking dish from the oven and let it cool for 5 minutes before serving.

FIVE-MINUTE BREAKFAST BANANA SPLITS

PREP TIME: **5 MINUTES**

SERVES 4

4 bananas

2 cups vanilla yogurt

1 cup fresh blueberries

1 cup fresh strawberries, sliced

1 cup pecans, almonds, or peanuts, chopped

VARIATION TIP: Top these healthy sundae-like breakfasts with anything you like. Think coconut, whipped cream, or cherries. Diced pineapple and shredded coconut make these banana splits tropical and fun for the summer. Top with chocolate chips or maple syrup if you're looking for a sweet treat. Top with granola for even more protein and fiber. Eliminate the nuts for those with an allergy.

Every kid (and kid at heart) will love these banana splits, because you can indulge without actually indulging. It's an all-around healthy breakfast treat: Bananas are loaded with potassium, the yogurt has protein, and the berries are packed with antioxidants, fiber, and nutrients. Use any yogurt you like: dairy, Greek, soy, cashew, Icelandic—the options are many and some allow you to make this recipe vegan and/or dairy-free. You, and your kids, will be clambering for this five-minute, five-ingredient delight.

1. Slice each banana lengthwise, and place the halves on either side of a shallow bowl, with one banana per bowl.

2. Spoon the yogurt on top of the bananas in the 4 bowls. Top the bananas and yogurt with the blueberries and strawberries. Then, sprinkle each banana split with chopped nuts and any other toppings you desire (see Variation Tip). Serve immediately.

FRESH BLUEBERRY, CREAM CHEESE, AND CINNAMON ROLLS

PREP TIME: **10 MINUTES**   COOK TIME: **18 MINUTES**

5-INGREDIENT, NUT-FREE, QUICK

SERVES 4

8 tablespoons unsalted butter

4 tablespoons packed light brown sugar

1 (12-ounce) tube cinnamon rolls

1 cup whipped cream cheese spread

2 cups fresh or thawed frozen blueberries

1 cup confectioners' sugar (optional)

VARIATION TIP: *Strawberries, peaches, or blackberries work well in place of the blueberries.*

INGREDIENT TIP: *A quick icing dresses these up a bit. To make, combine 2 cups of confectioners' sugar, 1 teaspoon of pure vanilla extract, and ¼ cup of milk. Either drizzle the icing on top or use as a dip.*

I am convinced that the only reason anyone ever invites me over for brunch is because they know I will bring these cinnamon rolls. The alluring aroma. The beckoning brown sugar–butter crust. The warm bursts of blueberry. Only the very strongest can resist. I always make a batch of icing for dipping, too (see the Ingredient Tip).

1. Preheat the oven to 375°F.

2. In a glass measuring cup, mix the butter and brown sugar, and heat in the microwave in 10-second increments until the butter is melted, stirring between each increment. Pour it into a 9-by-9-inch square baking dish.

3. Roll out the cinnamon-roll dough to about ¼ inch thick and scoop dollops of whipped cream cheese over each roll, then scatter the blueberries over the cream cheese.

4. Roll the dough back up and slice into 1-inch rolls.

5. Arrange the cinnamon rolls in a single layer over the melted butter and sugar.

6. Bake until the cinnamon rolls are lightly golden, about 17 minutes (check after 15 minutes so the dough doesn't burn).

7. Sift confectioners' sugar (if using) over the baked dish as a garnish.

BAKED CUSTARD FRUIT PANCAKES

PREP TIME: **10 MINUTES**   COOK TIME: **45 MINUTES**

NUT-FREE, OFF THE SHELF

SERVES 6

2 tablespoons unsalted butter, melted, plus more for greasing

¼ cup plus 3 tablespoons sugar, divided

3 large eggs

¾ cup whole milk

½ teaspoon cinnamon

½ teaspoon nutmeg

½ cup all-purpose flour

¼ teaspoon salt

3 cups frozen mixed berries

Maple syrup, for serving

VARIATION TIP: *Use almond or rice flour in place of the all-purpose flour to make a gluten-free version.*

Pancakes are a universal food, beloved worldwide. Practically every culture creates its own version, from crepes in France to blinis in Russia. And here is my version, although I do love a simple, traditional take as well. This recipe has minimal hands-on time, so you can get ready for your busy morning while these bake.

1. Preheat the oven to 350°F. Coat a 2-quart baking dish with butter, and dust the buttered dish with 3 tablespoons of the sugar.

2. In a blender, combine the eggs, milk, melted butter, remaining ¼ cup of sugar, cinnamon, and nutmeg, and blend until smooth.

3. Add the flour and salt, and pulse until blended.

4. Pour the egg batter into the buttered and sugared baking dish.

5. Sprinkle the frozen berries over the batter, spreading evenly.

6. Bake for 45 minutes, until the custard is puffed and the center is just barely set.

7. Allow it to set for 10 minutes before serving.

8. Lightly drizzle the custard with maple syrup just before serving.

COLORFUL BELL-PEPPER EGG RINGS

PREP TIME: **2 MINUTES**   COOK TIME: **10 MINUTES**

5-INGREDIENT, DAIRY-FREE, GLUTEN-FREE, NUT-FREE, QUICK

SERVES 4

1 red bell pepper

1 green bell pepper

1 orange bell pepper

1 tablespoon olive
oil, divided

8 large eggs

Salt

Freshly ground
black pepper

VARIATION TIP: *Use 1 cup
of egg whites instead
of the whole eggs for a
lower-calorie version.*

Did you know that red peppers pack the most nutrients because they spend the longest amount of time ripening on the vine? Green peppers have the fewest nutrients of the bell pepper color range, but still are excellent sources of vitamins B_6 and K. No matter the color, this recipe is a visual and flavorful surprise that is sure to impress any breakfast guest. I like to use red, green, and orange pepper rings, because each brings a different taste to the eggs.

1. Slice each pepper into ½-inch rings, removing the seeds and core. Cut 8 rings total.

2. In a large non-stick skillet, heat 1½ teaspoons of the oil over medium heat.

3. Place half of the pepper rings in the skillet in a single layer (you will have to do a second batch).

4. Crack one egg into each pepper ring, and sprinkle with salt and pepper to taste.

5. Cook the eggs until the whites are set and the yolks are still soft. Flip the egg-filled pepper rings, and cook another 45 to 60 seconds to set the egg yolks.

6. Repeat with the remaining 1½ teaspoons oil, pepper rings, and eggs, and serve immediately.

SAVORY AND SPICY BREAKFAST ENCHILADAS

PREP TIME: 5 MINUTES   **COOK TIME: 30 MINUTES**

SERVES 5

1 tablespoon extra-virgin olive oil

8 large eggs

½ teaspoon cayenne pepper

Salt

Freshly ground black pepper

1 cup diced frozen bell peppers

1 cup diced frozen onions

1 (15-ounce) can black beans, rinsed and drained

1 cup shredded cheddar cheese, divided

2 cups jarred enchilada sauce, divided

10 (7- to 8-inch) soft corn tortillas

Try this twist on a Mexican classic. These enchiladas are perfect for Sunday brunch, when you have a little more time to sit at the table and enjoy a leisurely meal. I like to serve avocado slices and sour cream on the side, along with a basket of tortilla chips to scoop up all the tasty enchilada bits.

1. Heat the oil in a large nonstick skillet over medium-high heat.

2. In a mixing bowl, beat the eggs with the cayenne and the salt and black pepper to taste. Set aside.

3. In the heated skillet, combine the peppers and onions, and cook about 3 minutes until thawed.

4. Pour the egg mixture into the skillet, stir with the peppers and onions, and let cook for 2 minutes. Add black beans to the eggs and slowly stir for another minute.

5. Remove the eggs from the heat and gently fold in ½ cup of the cheese.

6. Cover the bottom of a 9-by-13-inch baking dish with 1 cup of the enchilada sauce.

7. Lay a tortilla out on a cutting board and add ⅓ cup of the egg mixture to the center of the tortilla. Roll up the tortilla and place it seam-down into the enchilada sauce in the baking dish. Repeat with the remaining tortillas.

8. Pour the remaining enchilada sauce over the tortillas in the dish. Cover with aluminum foil, and bake for 14 minutes.

9. Remove the foil and sprinkle with the remaining ½ cup of cheese. Bake uncovered for 10 minutes, until the cheese has melted and the sauce is bubbly.

CHOCOLATE AND STRAWBERRY PUFF TARTS

PREP TIME: **10 MINUTES**   COOK TIME: **20 MINUTES**

QUICK

SERVES 6

½ cup strawberry
   jelly or jam

2 teaspoons cornstarch

1 large egg

1 tablespoon water

Flour, for dusting

2 sheets puff pastry,
   thawed (see Ingre-
   dient Tip)

½ cup milk choco-
   late chips

When I was young, Pop-Tarts were my favorite treat to take along for a walk on the beach. Still to this day, I associate the smell of salt water with the sweet toaster treat. Once I grew up and moved into my own apartment, my pantry was never without a box of strawberry frosted Pop-Tarts. While I still enjoy a warm Pop-Tart every now and then, I really enjoy making my own batch of homemade puff tarts, especially because I can pick the flavor. Enjoy these breakfast favorites on the go with a warm latte.

1. Preheat the oven to 375°F.

2. In a medium bowl, combine the jelly with the cornstarch.

3. In a separate medium bowl, whisk together the egg and water.

4. Lightly flour your work surface, then unroll one sheet of puff pastry. Cut each pastry sheet into 6 equal rectangles. Place 6 of the rectangles onto a baking sheet lined with parchment. Set aside the other 6 rectangles. Spread equal quantities of the jelly mixture in the center of each of the first 6 rectangles, leaving a ½-inch margin around the edges. Sprinkle an equal amount of chocolate chips on top.

5. Using a pastry brush, brush the egg mixture along the edge of each rectangle, then top with the remaining 6 pastry rectangles. Using a fork, gently press the sides of each rectangle to seal.

6. Brush the tart tops with the remaining egg mixture. Bake them until they turn golden brown, 15 to 20 minutes. Transfer the puff tarts to a cooling rack and let them cool slightly before serving.

VARIATION TIP: Don't forget the icing, if you want it. In a medium mixing bowl, combine 1 cup of confectioners' sugar, ½ teaspoon of pure vanilla extract, and 2 tablespoons of milk. Top with sprinkles for color.

INGREDIENT TIP: To thaw the puff pastry, wrap each piece of pastry with plastic wrap, and leave it in the refrigerator for 4 hours or overnight. Do not pull the pastry out of the refrigerator until you are ready to use it; you want to work with it while it is still cold.

VARIATION TIP: Substitute peanut butter or sunflower butter instead of the chocolate chips for a peanut butter and jelly version.

EGG AND AVOCADO TOAST

PREP TIME: **15 MINUTES**   COOK TIME: **5 MINUTES**

5-INGREDIENT, NUT-FREE, QUICK

SERVES 2

2 ripe avocados, halved and pitted

1 tablespoon lemon juice

4 slices multigrain bread, toasted

1 tablespoon white vinegar

4 large eggs

Salt

Freshly ground black pepper

VARIATION TIP: *Colorful, tangy pickled radish adds extra flair: Combine ½ cup of sliced radishes, 2 tablespoons of red wine vinegar, and 1 tablespoon of granulated sugar in a small bowl. Let it sit for 10 minutes, then drain and arrange on top of the avocado toast.*

I had the best avocado toast of my life at a little bakery in Salt Lake City. The dish was very simple, with just avocado, pickled radish, and a light sprinkle of everything bagel seasoning. The poached egg adds that extra protein pop and takes this dish from great to irresistible. There are so many variations on the avocado toast trend, but the pickled radish (see Variation Tip) makes it really special.

1. In a medium mixing bowl, combine the avocado flesh and lemon juice, and mash, leaving the avocado slightly chunky. Top each slice of toast with the mashed avocado.

2. Fill a large pot with four inches of water and add the vinegar. Bring to a gentle boil.

3. Crack each egg into a separate ramekin or small bowl (1 egg per ramekin or bowl).

4. Carefully slide each egg into the boiling water and leave untouched for 3 to 4 minutes until the whites are firm and the yolks are slightly runny.

5. Using a slotted spoon, remove each egg from the water and slide onto the avocado toast, one egg per piece of toast. Sprinkle with salt and pepper to taste.

INGREDIENT TIP: Choose an avocado that is dark green in color and slightly soft but not mushy. If you can only find avocados that are still bright green and very firm, store them in a brown paper bag at room temperature until the color changes and the avocados are slightly soft.

PEANUT BUTTER AND CHOCOLATE ELVIS SMOOTHIE

PREP TIME: **5 MINUTES**

5-INGREDIENT, NO COOK, OFF THE SHELF, ONE POT, QUICK

SERVES 2

2 ripe bananas

1 cup ice cubes

1½ cups milk

2 tablespoons
    peanut butter

2 tablespoons unsweet-
    ened cocoa powder

1 teaspoon pure
    vanilla extract

QUICK TIP: *Keep sliced bananas in the freezer for a quick addition to the blender.*

VARIATION TIPS: *Add spinach for a burst of iron or add frozen strawberries to add more of a peanut butter and jelly vibe. The peanut butter can be replaced with sunflower butter to accommodate nut allergies.*

MAKE IT VEGAN: *Use a nut or rice milk in place of dairy milk to make this recipe vegan.*

Elvis knew a good combo when he saw one: peanut butter and bananas. Here, the ingredients get "all shook up" in a blender to make a delicious and healthy smoothie. Peanut butter and milk add protein, bananas bring the potassium, and cocoa powder lends a chocolatey sweetness that make this smoothie difficult to pass up. It's so easy to add even more nutrients by sneaking in things like spinach or chia seeds.

In a blender, combine the bananas, ice, milk, peanut butter, cocoa powder, and vanilla, and blend at high speed until well mixed. Divide into two chilled glasses and serve immediately.

Almond-Butter Oatmeal Energy Bites, page 33

CHAPTER THREE

Snacks and Bites

—◇—

ROASTED-BROCCOLI HUMMUS

PREP TIME: **5 MINUTES**   COOK TIME: **15 MINUTES**

DAIRY-FREE, GLUTEN-FREE, NUT-FREE, QUICK

MAKES 2 CUPS

2 cups chopped broccoli

2 tablespoons plus ¼ cup extra-virgin olive oil, divided

3 garlic cloves, peeled and minced

1 (15.5-ounce) can chickpeas, drained and rinsed

Juice of 2 lemons

2 tablespoons tahini

VARIATION TIPS: *This recipe also works well with roasted carrots, cauliflower, or Brussels sprouts in place of the broccoli.*

INGREDIENT TIP: *Tahini, a sort of nut butter made out of sesame seeds, can be found in the international food aisle of most grocery stores. Although tahini is a traditional ingredient in hummus, you can leave it out of the recipe altogether for a nut-free version, or replace with ricotta cheese for a creamy broccoli dip.*

Hummus is the perfect snack and it's a crowd-pleaser at parties. It's easy to make, versatile in terms of dipping choices and add-ins, and a great source of protein, omega-3s, and numerous vitamins. If you've only ever bought hummus in the store, you're in for a real treat here. I love hummus as an afternoon pick-me-up with raw carrots, celery, or sugar snap peas. Hummus also makes a great spread for sandwiches in place of mayonnaise or mustard, or as a topping for baked potatoes.

1. Preheat the oven to 400°F. Line a baking sheet with parchment paper.

2. Put the broccoli in a single layer on the baking sheet, and drizzle with 2 tablespoons olive oil. Roast in the oven for 15 minutes, until the broccoli begins to brown.

3. In a food processor, combine the roasted broccoli, garlic, chickpeas, lemon juice, and tahini, and pulse until combined.

4. Slowly drizzle in the remaining ¼ cup of olive oil. Continue to process until the hummus is smooth.

CINNAMON SUGAR AND BANANA SAUTÉ

PREP TIME: **5 MINUTES**   COOK TIME: **6 MINUTES**

5-INGREDIENT, DAIRY-FREE, GLUTEN-FREE, NUT-FREE, OFF THE SHELF, ONE-POT

SERVES 4

4 bananas

1 tablespoon olive oil

1 tablespoon ground cinnamon

1 tablespoon granulated sugar

2 tablespoons honey, for drizzling (optional)

MAKE IT VEGAN: *Omit the honey or use maple syrup instead to make this recipe vegan.*

Although bananas are great just as they are, they are extra delicious pan seared and tossed with a little cinnamon and sugar. It's a great midday snack for energy and satisfies a sweet tooth without resorting to junk food. I like to drizzle honey on warm banana slices for a little more flavor and sweetness. These bananas are also an excellent topping for ice cream and oatmeal.

1. Peel the bananas and slice them into ¼-inch rounds.

2. In a large skillet, heat the olive oil over medium-high heat. Add the bananas, and sprinkle with the cinnamon and sugar. Cook for 3 minutes, then flip and cook another 3 minutes. The bananas are done when they begin to brown.

3. Remove the bananas from the heat, and drizzle with honey, if using, before serving.

TARRAGON-MARINATED BRUSSELS SPROUTS

PREP TIME: 5 MINUTES, PLUS 10 TO 24 HOURS CHILLING IN THE REFRIGERATOR
COOK TIME: 7 MINUTES

DAIRY-FREE, GLUTEN-FREE, NUT-FREE, OFF THE SHELF, VEGAN

SERVES 6

1 (16-ounce) package frozen Brussels sprouts

1 (16-ounce) package frozen mixed vegetables

1 cup tarragon vinegar (see Ingredient Tip)

¾ cup extra-virgin olive oil

4 garlic cloves, minced

1 tablespoon sugar

1 tablespoon salt

1 teaspoon hot sauce

INGREDIENT TIP: *If you are not able to find tarragon vinegar, use white wine vinegar and sprinkle 2 tablespoons of dried tarragon into the marinade.*

VARIATION TIP: *The original recipe that was handed down to me used vegetable oil instead of olive oil. I prefer olive oil because of its flavor and health benefits, but vegetable oil will work just as well.*

This is probably my favorite recipe in the world, and the reason why I love Brussels sprouts today as much as I do. I have been eating these marinated Brussels sprouts since I was young, and I am rarely without a batch in my refrigerator as an adult. These are perfect for a picnic or potluck get-together. The Brussels sprouts and veggies are not only crunchy but they are also bursting with the tangy flavor of the tarragon vinegar. In other words, they bring an entirely new meaning to the command "Eat your Brussels sprouts."

1. Cook the Brussels sprouts and mixed vegetables according to package directions, and drain well. You want the Brussels sprouts to be fully cooked.

2. In a medium bowl, mix together the vinegar, olive oil, garlic, sugar, salt, and hot sauce to create the marinade.

3. Add the cooked Brussels sprouts and veggies to the marinade and let them sit in the refrigerator for 10 to 24 hours.

ALMOND-BUTTER OATMEAL ENERGY BITES

PREP TIME: **5 MINUTES, PLUS 20 MINUTES CHILLING IN THE REFRIGERATOR**

NO COOK, OFF THE SHELF, ONE POT, QUICK

SERVES 6

½ cup almond butter

1 cup old-fashioned oats

½ cup chocolate chips

⅓ cup pure maple syrup

½ cup ground flaxseed

1 tablespoon chia seeds

1 teaspoon pure vanilla
or almond extract

Unsweetened shred-
ded coconut and/or
crushed pistachios, for
rolling (optional)

VARIATION TIP: *Peanut
butter or sunflower butter
work very well in place of
the almond butter.*

MAKE IT VEGAN: *Replace
the chocolate chips with
vegan chocolate chips
or nuts.*

Don't say I didn't warn you: These are seriously addic-
tive. But it's okay, because they are an all-natural,
energy-lifting treat. I enjoy these with a cup of lic-
orice tea or a glass of almond milk for an afternoon
pick-me-up. In the fall, I like to add a teaspoon
of pumpkin pie spice to the mixture for a nutritious
pumpkin spice snack. Or try adding hot chocolate
powder and peppermint extract to give as gifts for
the holidays.

1. In a mixing bowl, combine the almond butter, oats,
   chocolate chips, maple syrup, flaxseed, chia seeds, and
   vanilla extract. Mix and cover with plastic wrap.

2. Put the bowl in the refrigerator for 20 minutes.

3. Roll the chilled dough into bite-sized balls. Place the
   coconut and/or pistachios, if using, in separate shallow
   bowls, and roll the balls in the toppings, pressing
   gently to adhere.

ROASTED GARLIC-PARMESAN CARROT FRIES

PREP TIME: **5 MINUTES**   COOK TIME: **20 MINUTES**

5-INGREDIENT, GLUTEN-FREE, NUT-FREE, OFF THE SHELF, QUICK

SERVES 4

8 carrots

2 tablespoons olive oil

½ cup grated Parmesan cheese

2 teaspoons garlic powder

INGREDIENT TIP: *Baby carrots do not work well in this recipe due to their plumpness. It's best to buy whole carrots and cut them into equal-size pieces.*

One of my favorite reasons to go to the farmers' market is the fry guy who serves up delicious hot and crispy fries dripping in garlic and Parmesan cheese. It's a perfect, portable snack in a cup. At home, I do a healthy twist, almost equally delicious, using carrots and roasting them instead of frying. These are perfect alongside black bean or veggie burgers. Sprinkle with fresh parsley, if desired, for a little pop of color.

1. Preheat the oven to 400°F, and line a baking sheet with parchment paper.

2. Peel and cut the carrots into sticks that are about ¼ inch thick and 1 inch long, as consistently as you can. Stab a fork into the carrot to stabilize it as you cut. This will prevent the carrot from rolling and slipping under the knife.

3. In a mixing bowl, toss the carrots with the olive oil, cheese, and garlic powder. Spread the carrots on the baking sheet in a single layer.

4. Roast the carrots for 20 minutes, stirring halfway through. Let the carrots cool for a few minutes before serving.

EVERYTHING BAGEL–CHEESE CRISPS

PREP TIME: 5 MINUTES   **COOK TIME: 5 MINUTES**

5-INGREDIENT, GLUTEN-FREE, QUICK

MAKES 12 CRISPS

1 cup shredded
Parmesan cheese

2 tablespoons olive oil

2 tablespoons every-
thing bagel seasoning,
for sprinkling

VARIATION TIP: *These
are equally delicious with
sharp or extra-sharp cheddar cheese.*

These are one of the easiest snacks you will ever make.
Cheese crisps make an excellent topping on salads and
in soups; crumble the crisps onto baked potatoes, on
burgers, or in a taco for an unexpected twist. I even love
to eat these cheese crisps on their own, with oregano in
place of the everything bagel seasoning.

1. Preheat the oven to 400°F. Line a baking sheet with
   parchment paper.

2. In a mixing bowl, combine the cheese and oil. Using
   tongs, toss the cheese until it is coated in the oil.

3. Put the cheese mixture on the baking sheet,
   1 tablespoon at a time, placing each spoonful about
   1 inch apart.

4. Sprinkle everything bagel seasoning over the
   cheese crisps.

5. Bake for 5 minutes, or until the crisps are golden. Let
   them cool for 5 minutes before serving.

BROCCOLI-RICOTTA TOTS

PREP TIME: **15 MINUTES**   COOK TIME: **14 MINUTES**

NUT-FREE, QUICK

SERVES 6

Cooking spray

2 cups chopped broccoli

1 garlic clove, peeled
and minced

¼ cup plus
3 tablespoons
all-purpose flour

½ teaspoon
baking powder

2 large eggs

¼ cup plain
bread crumbs

½ cup full-fat
ricotta cheese

1 cup warm marinara
sauce, for dipping

VARIATION TIP: *Replace the
broccoli with cauliflower for
cauliflower-ricotta tots (the
color may make it easier
to hide the veggie). Use
gluten-free bread crumbs
and rice flour instead of
all-purpose flour to make
this recipe gluten-free.*

I often get asked how to hide vegetables in recipes so
parents can sneak some extra nutrients into food for
their kids. These cheesy tots are so delicious, you might
be able to sneak that broccoli right past them. And if
you can, they'll receive an infusion of fiber, multiple
vitamins and minerals, like vitamin C and calcium, and
antioxidants. For another recipe with hidden vegetables,
check out the Chocolate-Beet Brownies (page 111).

1. Preheat the oven to 450°F. Line a large baking sheet
   with parchment paper, and spray it with cooking spray.

2. In a food processor, combine the broccoli, garlic, flour,
   and baking powder, and pulse until roughly chopped.

3. Add the eggs and pulse a few times to mix. Add the
   bread crumbs and ricotta cheese, and pulse again until
   the ingredients are blended.

4. Drop a tablespoon of broccoli mixture one at a time
   onto the prepared baking sheet, about 1 inch apart. Do
   not flatten them. Bake for 6 to 7 minutes.

5. Flip and bake another 6 to 7 minutes until golden
   brown. Serve with warm marinara sauce for dipping.

SALT-AND-VINEGAR ROASTED CHICKPEAS

PREP TIME: **20 MINUTES**   COOK TIME: **25 MINUTES**

5-INGREDIENT, DAIRY-FREE, GLUTEN-FREE, NUT-FREE, OFF THE SHELF, VEGAN

SERVES 4

2 (15.5-ounce) cans chickpeas, drained and rinsed

2 cups white distilled vinegar

Sea salt, to taste

INGREDIENT TIP: *Some of the chickpeas will pop and jump in the oven. Do not be alarmed if you hear a popping sound, and be careful pulling the pan out of the oven because some of the chickpeas will still be hot enough to pop and jump.*

Salt-and-vinegar potato chips used to be my favorite indulgence. But a girl can't live on potato chips alone. These salt-and-vinegar roasted chickpeas satisfy those salty, tangy, and crunchy cravings without sacrificing your health. Chickpeas have protein and soluble fiber, enough to hold you over until the next meal. They also make a great side dish.

1. Preheat the oven to 400°F. Line a baking sheet with parchment paper.

2. In a saucepan, combine the chickpeas and vinegar, and bring to a boil. Remove from the heat and let them soak for 15 minutes.

3. Drain the chickpeas and put them in a single layer on the prepared baking sheet. Sprinkle with the sea salt. Roast the chickpeas for 15 minutes, shake the pan, and then roast another 5 to 10 minutes, until the chickpeas are golden brown.

NACHO POPCORN

PREP TIME: **5 MINUTES**

DAIRY-FREE, GLUTEN-FREE, NO COOK, NUT-FREE, OFF THE SHELF,
ONE POT, QUICK, VEGAN

SERVES 6

6 cups freshly
popped popcorn

Olive oil spray

2 tablespoons nutri-
tional yeast

1 teaspoon salt

½ teaspoon cay-
enne pepper

½ teaspoon
onion powder

½ teaspoon
garlic powder

Forget the movie-theater variety, discard the
chemical-lined microwave types, and make your own
seasoned popcorn. If you have an air popper, this is
the perfect time to break it out—or try the super-easy
microwave method in the Ingredient Tip. I make
the spice mix in a large batch and keep it in a shaker
next to my spices to have at the ready whenever an
impromptu movie night pops up. When I make the
popcorn, I just spray it with olive oil and sprinkle the
spice mix over top.

1. Pour all of the popcorn into a large bowl and lightly
   spray it with the olive oil spray.

2. Sprinkle on the nutritional yeast, salt, cayenne pepper,
   onion powder, and garlic powder, and mix thoroughly
   into the popcorn to coat. Serve while warm.

INGREDIENT TIP: To make super-easy, additive-free microwave popcorn, pour ¼ cup of popcorn kernels into a brown
paper lunch bag, then fold over the top of the bag once or
twice. Cook on high in a microwave about 2 minutes or until
the popping slows.

Mediterranean-Inspired Couscous Bowls, page 56

CHAPTER FOUR

Soups, Sandwiches, and Salads

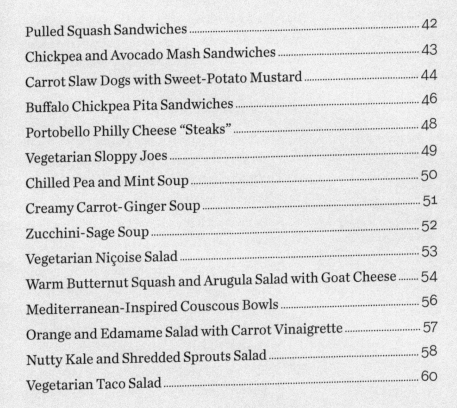

PULLED SQUASH SANDWICHES

PREP TIME: 10 MINUTES   **COOK TIME: 45 MINUTES**

5-INGREDIENT, DAIRY-FREE, NUT-FREE, VEGAN

SERVES 4

1 medium to large spa-
   ghetti squash

1 tablespoon olive oil

Salt

1 tablespoon
   smoked paprika

3 tablespoons dark
   brown sugar

½ cup barbecue sauce

4 hoagie rolls

Bread and butter pickle
   slices, for garnish
   (optional)

VARIATION TIP: *You can
skip the roll and use the
pulled squash as a topping
for a salad or even in a taco.*

This recipe is inspired by one of my favorite restaurants in Charleston, South Carolina, called Butcher and Bee. They used to post their daily menu on a chalkboard and "pulled squash" sandwiches were one of their fan favorites. Spaghetti squash is a great choice for a pulled plant-based sandwich; I like it more than jackfruit (which is often the veg go-to for pulled sandwiches) because the squash offers iron and vitamin A and does not have as much sugar.

1. Preheat the oven to 375°F.

2. Cut the squash in half lengthwise and scoop out the seeds. Place the squash halves in a baking dish, cut-side up. Brush the flesh with the olive oil. Sprinkle the squash with the salt to taste, smoked paprika, and brown sugar.

3. Bake the squash in the oven for 40 minutes or until golden brown. Leave the oven on.

4. Remove the squash from the oven and let it cool enough to handle. Using a spoon, gently scrape out the flesh of the squash into a medium bowl. The squash should separate into strings. Gently toss the squash with the barbecue sauce.

5. Split the rolls in half and put them in the oven for 5 minutes, until the edges are toasted brown. Top one half of each of the rolls with the squash, garnish with bread and butter pickles, if using, and sandwich with the other roll half.

CHICKPEA AND AVOCADO MASH SANDWICHES

PREP TIME: 10 MINUTES

5-INGREDIENT, DAIRY-FREE, GLUTEN-FREE, NO COOK, NUT-FREE, QUICK, VEGAN

SERVES 4

2 (15-ounce) cans chickpeas, drained and rinsed

3 avocados, halved and pitted

Juice from 1 large lemon

Salt

Freshly ground black pepper

8 slices bread, toasted if desired

This is so quick and easy, and it's packed with protein, healthy fats, and even a little vitamin C. I like to toast the bread and add more vegetables, like tomatoes and alfalfa sprouts, to add some crunch and even more nutrients. You could also use the mash as a topping for tacos and rice bowls, like the Vegetarian Taco Salad (page 60) or the One-Pot Rice and Bean Casserole (page 70).

1. In a mixing bowl, mash the chickpeas with a fork or potato masher, leaving them slightly chunky.

2. Scoop the avocado flesh into the bowl with the chickpeas and add the lemon juice. Sprinkle with salt and pepper to taste. Mash ingredients together until mostly smooth.

3. Divide the mash among four slices of bread and top with remaining bread.

CARROT SLAW DOGS WITH SWEET-POTATO MUSTARD

PREP TIME: **15 MINUTES**   COOK TIME: **15 MINUTES**

NUT-FREE, QUICK

MAKES 6 DOGS

2 large sweet potatoes

¾ cup blue-cheese crumbles

2 cups prepared coleslaw

2 tablespoons olive oil

4 cups shredded carrots

Salt

Freshly ground black pepper

2 teaspoons garlic powder

3 tablespoons Dijon mustard

2 tablespoons water

1 tablespoon apple cider vinegar

6 hot dog buns

INGREDIENT TIP: *I like to save time by buying prepared coleslaw straight from the deli section of my grocery store. Use the extra sweet-potato mustard on sandwiches, with grilled vegetables, or for dipping fries.*

Just outside Charleston, South Carolina, there's a cult-favorite restaurant called Jack's Cosmic Dogs. It's another place I go anytime I find myself in the Charleston area, and my order is the same every visit: Three Bunny in a Bun "Dogs"—it's shredded carrots, blue-cheese slaw, and sweet-potato mustard. Use the leftover mustard on the Carrot and White-Bean Veggie Burger (page 78), or as a dip for the Roasted Garlic–Parmesan Carrot Fries (page 34).

1. Wash and pierce the sweet potatoes 3 or 4 times with a fork. Put them on a plate and cook them in the microwave on high for 5 minutes, turning halfway through, so they can be easily pierced with a paring knife. Cut the potatoes open lengthwise and let them cool.

2. In a medium mixing bowl, fold the blue-cheese crumbles into the coleslaw, and set aside.

3. In a skillet, heat the oil over medium-high heat. Add the carrots, salt and pepper to taste, and garlic powder, and stir together. Continue to cook for 7 minutes, until the carrots begin to soften slightly, stirring occasionally.

4. While the carrots cook, scoop out the flesh of the sweet potatoes into a food processor. Add the mustard and pulse until blended. Add the water and continue to pulse until it reaches a creamy consistency, adding more water 1 tablespoon at a time, if needed. Bonus: This yields more mustard than you will need for just this recipe.

5. Remove the carrots from the heat and add the apple cider vinegar, stirring well to mix.

6. On the hot dog buns, spread the sweet-potato mustard on one half. Divide the shredded carrot mixture evenly among the buns, and top each bun with the blue-cheese coleslaw.

BUFFALO CHICKPEA
PITA SANDWICHES

PREP TIME: 20 MINUTES **COOK TIME: 5 MINUTES**

DAIRY-FREE, NUT-FREE, QUICK, VEGAN

SERVES 4

For the blue-cheese dressing

½ teaspoon
garlic powder

½ cup vegan mayonnaise

1 teaspoon lemon juice

1 teaspoon apple
cider vinegar

¼ teaspoon tahini

¼ cup crumbled
extra-firm tofu

*For the buffalo chickpea
pitas*

3 tablespoons hot sauce

2 tablespoons
extra-virgin olive oil

2 teaspoons
garlic powder

2 (15-ounce) cans
chickpeas, rinsed
and drained

4 pita bread rounds,
slit at top

1 cup shredded lettuce

¼ cup finely
minced celery

3 tablespoons finely
chopped fresh parsley

There's a reason why hot sauce and blue-cheese dressing pair so well together: The creaminess of the dressing tones down the heat in the hot sauce, so that just when your mouth is screaming "no!" the dressing comes in and saves the day. The dressing recipe makes more than you'll need for this dish, but that's to your advantage because it's the perfect topping for salads, such as the Vegetarian Niçoise Salad (page 53), or as a dip for the Roasted Garlic–Parmesan Carrot Fries (page 34).

1. **To make the blue-cheese dressing:** In a medium bowl, mix the garlic powder, mayonnaise, lemon juice, vinegar, and tahini until you have a nice, creamy, dressing-like consistency. Crumble the tofu into the dressing mixture to resemble blue cheese crumbles. Cover and store in the refrigerator until ready to use; it will last up to 1 week.

2. **To make the pitas:** In a medium bowl, combine the hot sauce, olive oil, and garlic powder, and mix well. Add the chickpeas and toss or stir to coat with the sauce.

3. Heat a skillet or saucepan over medium heat and add the chickpeas. Sauté over medium heat for about 5 minutes, or until heated through, stirring frequently. Remove from the heat, and set aside to cool slightly.

4. In another bowl, toss the lettuce and blue-cheese dressing together. Divide and stuff the lettuce mixture into each pita. Mix the celery and parsley into the slightly cooled chickpea mixture, and spoon the mixture into the pita pockets with the lettuce.

QUICK TIP: Buy bottled blue cheese or ranch dressing instead of making the dressing in this recipe. It will not be vegan or dairy-free, but it will save time.

INGREDIENT TIP: A dollop of tahini paste adds a tangy twist and works as a binder in the blue-cheese dressing. Tahini is found in the international food aisle of grocery stores. It's a mashed sesame paste and is a staple in hummus.

PORTOBELLO PHILLY CHEESE "STEAKS"

PREP TIME: **10 MINUTES**   COOK TIME: **10 MINUTES**

ONE POT, QUICK

SERVES 4

2 tablespoons olive oil

2 cups sliced
  green pepper

2 cups sliced onion

2 teaspoons
  garlic powder

Salt

Freshly ground
  black pepper

4 extra-large porto-
  bello mushrooms,
  thickly sliced

3 tablespoons red
  wine vinegar

4 slices provo-
  lone cheese

4 sub rolls, split
  lengthwise

VARIATION TIP: *Though
it isn't necessary, some
people prefer to remove
the gills from the underside
of the mushroom before
using. Simply use a spoon to
gently scrape the gills out.*

Ask 50 Philadelphians where to get the best cheesesteak, and you will get 50 different answers. Pat's and Geno's, across the street from one another in South Philadelphia, still seem to be battling it out as the most famous. But never discount Steve's, Joe's, or John's, which all have multitudes of loyal followers. Philadelphia has not left vegetarians in the lurch, however, boasting some great places to find this delicacy, vegetarian-style. Though many use seitan in place of the steak, portobello mush-rooms (used here) work just as well, bringing a different flavor profile and different health benefits.

1. In a large skillet, heat the oil over medium-high heat. Add the green peppers, onions, and garlic powder. Sprinkle with salt and pepper to taste. Cook for about 5 minutes, stirring occasionally, until the vegetables begin to soften.

2. Add the mushrooms and red wine vinegar, reduce the heat to low, and let simmer for 5 minutes.

3. Evenly top the vegetables with the cheese and let them sit until the cheese begins to melt. Do not stir or mix.

4. Scoop ¼ of the cheesy vegetables into each of the sub rolls. Serve immediately.

VEGETARIAN SLOPPY JOES

PREP TIME: **10 MINUTES**   COOK TIME: **15 MINUTES**

DAIRY-FREE, NUT-FREE, ONE POT, QUICK, VEGAN

SERVES 6

2 tablespoons
  extra-virgin olive oil

1 cup diced white onion

½ cup diced celery

½ cup diced
  green pepper

2 garlic cloves, peeled
  and minced

1 (6-ounce) can
  tomato paste

2 tablespoons
  brown sugar

1 tablespoon apple
  cider vinegar

1 teaspoon dry mustard

½ teaspoon salt

1 cup water

2 (15-ounce) cans
  red kidney beans,
  drained and rinsed,
  slightly mashed

6 hamburger buns,
  toasted if desired

Sloppy Joes were always a quick go-to meal in my house growing up. And while nothing is faster than dumping a can of something into a pan and heating it up, I like to make my own sauce so I can control the salt, sugar, and preservatives. This is a fairly quick and easy recipe that replaces meat with red kidney beans, which are also full of protein.

1. Heat the oil in a large skillet over medium heat, and add the onion, celery, green pepper, and garlic. Sauté until softened, about 5 minutes.

2. Add the tomato paste and stir well to combine.

3. Add the brown sugar, vinegar, dry mustard, and salt, and stir to combine well.

4. Add the water and the kidney beans and continue to cook an additional 5 minutes until the beans are heated through and most of the water is evaporated.

5. Divide the sloppy-Joe mixture among the hamburger buns and serve immediately.

CHILLED PEA AND MINT SOUP

PREP TIME: **10 MINUTES, PLUS 30 MINUTES CHILLING TIME**
COOK TIME: **15 MINUTES**

5-INGREDIENT, GLUTEN-FREE, NUT-FREE, ONE POT

SERVES 6

2 tablespoons olive oil

3 leeks, chopped, white and light green parts only

4 cups low-sodium vegetable broth

1 (20-ounce) package frozen sweet green peas

¼ cup fresh mint leaves

½ cup plain yogurt

INGREDIENT TIP: *After you cut the leeks, submerge them in a bowl of cold water for a few minutes to remove any residual dirt. Because of their large outer leaves, leeks tend to hold on to dirt and debris more than other vegetables.*

MAKE IT VEGAN: *Use a dairy-free version of the plain yogurt to make it vegan.*

Tiffany's, the famous jewelry store on 5th Avenue in Manhattan, briefly had a restaurant called the Blue Box Café. It literally allowed guests to enjoy "Breakfast at Tiffany's." They also allowed guests to enjoy lunch at Tiffany's, which featured this chilled pea and mint soup on the menu. I pared down my version of the recipe to make it quick and easy. It's delicious topped with Salt-and-Vinegar Roasted Chickpeas (page 37).

1. In a stockpot, heat the oil over medium-high heat. Add the leeks and cook about 7 minutes, stirring occasionally, until tender.

2. Add the vegetable broth and increase the heat to high to bring the soup to a boil.

3. Add the frozen peas and continue to cook over high heat for 3 to 4 minutes, until the peas are tender.

4. Remove the soup from the heat, then stir in the mint and yogurt.

5. Using an immersion blender, puree the soup until smooth. (You can also puree the soup in a blender in batches; just be sure to leave the lid a tiny bit ajar and wrap it in a kitchen towel to avoid splattering the soup or shattering the blender from the heat.)

6. Chill the soup in the refrigerator for at least 30 minutes, or until ready to enjoy. The soup will last about 4 days in an airtight container kept in the refrigerator.

CREAMY CARROT-GINGER SOUP

PREP TIME: **10 MINUTES**   COOK TIME: **25 MINUTES**

DAIRY-FREE, GLUTEN-FREE, NUT-FREE, ONE POT, VEGAN

SERVES 4

1 tablespoon olive oil

3 scallions, white and green parts, coarsely chopped

2 tablespoons peeled and minced fresh ginger

3 garlic cloves, minced

Salt

Freshly ground black pepper

7 carrots, peeled and chopped

1 (14-ounce) can full-fat coconut milk

1 (15-ounce) can cannellini beans, undrained

3 cups low-sodium vegetable broth

My mother made the best cream of carrot soup when I was growing up. She served it at every Thanksgiving dinner, and every special occasion. But this was no quick, light soup. It took time and lots of heavy cream. For the more health (and time) conscious, I have ditched the heavy cream (along with some of the unnecessary steps) to create this healthier, easier version.

1. In a stockpot, heat the olive oil over medium-high heat.

2. Add the scallions, ginger, and garlic. Stir for 2 minutes, until the mixture becomes fragrant. Season with salt and pepper to taste. Add the carrots, coconut milk, cannellini beans with their liquid, and broth.

3. Bring the mixture to a boil over high heat, then reduce the heat to low, and simmer for 20 minutes, stirring occasionally, until the carrots are tender.

4. Using an immersion blender, puree the soup until smooth. You can also puree the soup in a blender in batches; just be sure to leave the lid a tiny bit ajar and wrap it in a kitchen towel to avoid splattering the soup or shattering the blender from the heat. Serve immediately.

ZUCCHINI-SAGE SOUP

PREP TIME: **5 MINUTES**   COOK TIME: **20 MINUTES**

SERVES 4

2 tablespoons olive oil

6 celery stalks, chopped

2 cups chopped radishes

4 medium to large zuc-
    chinis, chopped

3 cups vegetable broth

2 teaspoons dried sage

2 teaspoons paprika

2 teaspoons chopped
    fresh thyme

Fresh sage leaves,
    for garnish

VARIATION TIP: *Replace
the zucchini with 3½ cups
of chopped broccoli for a
healthy broccoli soup.*

Zucchini is often overlooked and underrated, but it
is one of the few vegetables that can be found fresh
year-round in most regions, is incredibly versatile, and
is rich in vitamin A and antioxidants. This soup gives
zucchini its moment to shine. The radishes add an
unexpected hint of a peppery spice. A side of crusty
bread makes this a full meal.

1. In a stockpot, heat the oil over medium-high heat.
    Add the celery, radishes, and zucchini, and stir for
    5 minutes, until the vegetables begin to soften.

2. Add the vegetable broth, and simmer, stirring occa-
    sionally, for 10 minutes.

3. Add the dried sage, paprika, and fresh thyme, and
    simmer for 5 more minutes.

4. Using an immersion blender, puree the soup until
    smooth. You can also puree the soup in a blender in
    batches; just be sure to leave the lid a tiny bit ajar and
    wrap it in a kitchen towel to avoid splattering the soup
    or shattering the blender from the heat.

5. Garnish with fresh sage, and serve immediately.

VEGETARIAN NIÇOISE SALAD

PREP TIME: **10 MINUTES**   COOK TIME: **15 MINUTES**

DAIRY-FREE, GLUTEN-FREE, NUT-FREE, QUICK

SERVES 6

1 pound baby red
  potatoes

¼ cup red wine vinegar

1 (15-ounce) can
  chickpeas, drained
  and rinsed

2 tablespoons
  lemon juice

1 teaspoon chopped
  fresh dill

6 cups chopped romaine
  lettuce leaves

6 large hard-boiled eggs,
  peeled and quartered

2 cups halved cherry
  tomatoes

1 pound fresh green
  beans, trimmed
  and chopped

½ cup pitted Kala-
  mata olives

Balsamic vinegar,
  for serving

Salt

Freshly ground
  black pepper

Traditionally, a French Niçoise salad has canned tuna, potatoes, green beans, and Niçoise olives. There are so many different takes on the original that it's only right to have a vegetarian version here. I found Niçoise olives elusive in most grocery stores, so I replaced them here with equally tangy Kalamata olives. Instead of using canned tuna, use chickpeas tossed in lemon juice and dill for that fresh vegetarian spin. I like to buy hard-boiled eggs for added convenience, but you can also boil your own.

1. In a medium pot, cook the potatoes by adding enough water to cover them and bringing it to a boil. Let them simmer for 10 minutes, until the potatoes are tender. Drain the potatoes, drizzle with the red wine vinegar, and let them cool. Halve the potatoes.

2. While the potatoes are boiling, in a mixing bowl, combine the drained chickpeas, lemon juice, and fresh dill. Set aside.

3. Spread 1 cup of lettuce on each of 6 serving plates and arrange the potatoes, eggs, tomatoes, green beans, and olives in separate piles on top of the lettuce. Spoon the chickpea mixture into the middle of the lettuce.

4. Drizzle with balsamic vinegar to taste, and sprinkle with salt and pepper to taste.

WARM BUTTERNUT SQUASH AND ARUGULA SALAD WITH GOAT CHEESE

PREP TIME: **15 MINUTES**   COOK TIME: **5 MINUTES**

GLUTEN-FREE, QUICK

SERVES 4

For the vinaigrette

¾ cup white bal-
    samic vinegar

1 cup extra-virgin
    olive oil

2 teaspoons
    Dijon mustard

2 teaspoons
    minced garlic

1 minced shallot

¼ teaspoon salt

For the salad

2 tablespoons olive oil

4 cups butternut
    squash spirals
    (see Ingredient Tip)

Salt

Freshly ground
    black pepper

4 cups arugula

½ cup pepitas

2 cups diced fresh
    tomatoes

½ cup crumbled
    goat cheese

When the sweaters come out, this becomes one of my favorite lunches. This dish just brings out the feeling of crunching leaves, hay rides, and that first chill in the air. Goat cheese adds a tangy flavor that balances the spicy arugula and earthy butternut squash. Letting the squash cool for just 5 minutes prevents the arugula from wilting when you add the squash to the salad. It's still a warm salad for a cool day, though.

1. **To make the vinaigrette**: In a jar with a tight-closing lid, combine the vinegar, oil, mustard, garlic, shallot, and salt. Seal the jar, and shake vigorously until the vinaigrette is blended well.

2. **To make the salad**: In a skillet, heat the olive oil over medium heat. Add the butternut squash and sprinkle with salt and pepper to taste. Cook for 5 minutes, stirring occasionally, until tender. Remove from the heat and let it cool for 5 minutes.

3. As the squash cooks and cools, in a large mixing bowl, combine the arugula, pepitas, and tomatoes. Add the vinaigrette to the arugula mixture and toss well.

4. Add the still-warm squash to the bowl with the arugula and sprinkle with the goat cheese. Serve immediately.

INGREDIENT TIP: If you cannot find fresh butternut squash spirals in the produce section of your grocery store, check the frozen vegetables section. If using frozen spirals, just prepare them in the microwave according to the package directions and skip the stovetop instructions. However, you can also make your own spirals using a vegetable spiralizer, which can be found at most kitchen stores. Just peel the neck of the squash and run it through the spiralizer.

VARIATION TIP: Replace the squash with zucchini or beet spirals.

MEDITERRANEAN-INSPIRED COUSCOUS BOWLS

PREP TIME: **10 MINUTES**   COOK TIME: **15 MINUTES**

NUT-FREE, QUICK

SERVES 4

2 cups vegetable broth or water

1 tablespoon butter

2 cups dry couscous

½ cup extra-virgin olive oil

¼ cup lemon juice or red wine vinegar

2 cups chopped tomatoes

2 cups sliced cucumbers

2 cups crumbled feta cheese

1 red onion, sliced

1 (15-ounce) can chickpeas, drained and rinsed

1 cup dried cranberries

2 tablespoons fresh basil leaves

Couscous is a North African staple, meaning "well-rolled." It is made from semolina, wheat flour, and water, so it's actually a pasta, not a grain. But it makes the perfect base for a warm or cool Mediterranean-inspired bowl, and is a great alternative to a rice bowl. These bowls are quick and easy to prepare, have all of the nutrients you need in a healthy meal, and, most important, taste fantastic.

1. In a large saucepan, bring the vegetable broth and butter to a boil. Add the couscous and cover tightly with a lid. Remove it from the heat, and let it sit, covered, for 5 minutes.

2. In a mixing bowl, whisk together the oil and lemon juice. Pour the dressing into the couscous and mix well.

3. Divide the couscous among 4 serving bowls. Top with tomatoes, cucumbers, feta cheese, onion, chickpeas, and dried cranberries. Sprinkle with the torn basil leaves and serve immediately.

QUICK TIP: Buy vinaigrette to use in place of the extra-virgin olive oil and lemon juice.

MAKE IT VEGAN: Replace the butter with olive oil and omit the feta cheese. This will also make it dairy-free.

ORANGE AND EDAMAME SALAD WITH CARROT VINAIGRETTE

PREP TIME: 10 MINUTES

DAIRY-FREE, NO COOK, NUT-FREE, QUICK, VEGAN

SERVES 4

For the carrot vinaigrette

2 cups carrot juice

1 cup olive oil

3 teaspoons white wine vinegar

½ teaspoon salt

½ teaspoon ground cumin

1 teaspoon minced fresh ginger

For the salad

1 (12-ounce) package frozen shelled eda-mame, thawed

1 cup orange juice

4 cups spring mix or chopped romaine lettuce

2 scallions, white and green parts, sliced

2 cups mandarin orange segments

Crispy wonton or crispy rice noodles, for gar-nish (optional)

While on a trip to Cleveland, I stopped inside the famed West Side Market and found a vendor selling various flavored vinaigrettes. I bought a few different bottles and tried them at my hotel room later that night. I returned the next day and bought four more bottles of the carrot vinaigrette. It was so fresh and light, and I used it on everything from roasted vegetables to salads to rice bowls. Since I don't live in Cleveland, I had to figure out how to make my own.

1. **To make the carrot vinaigrette:** In a jar, combine the carrot juice, olive oil, vinegar, salt, cumin, and ginger. Seal with a tight-fitting lid, and shake to combine.

2. **To make the salad:** In a mixing bowl, combine the edamame and orange juice. Set aside.

3. Divide the lettuce among 4 serving plates. Top with the scallions and orange segments.

4. Drain the edamame (discarding the orange juice), and divide it among the salad plates.

5. Drizzle with the carrot vinaigrette to taste and sprinkle with crispy wonton noodles, if using.

NUTTY KALE AND SHREDDED SPROUTS SALAD

PREP TIME: **10 MINUTES**

SERVES 4

For the vinaigrette

¼ cup fresh lemon juice

1 tablespoon
   Dijon mustard

¼ cup extra-virgin
   olive oil

Salt

Freshly ground
   black pepper

*For the cheesy sprinkle
topping*

½ cup raw almonds

½ cup raw cashews

¼ cup nutritional yeast

½ teaspoon sea salt

¼ teaspoon
   garlic powder

For the salad

3 cups coarsely chopped
   curly kale, stems
   removed and discarded

3 tablespoons
   extra-virgin olive oil

1 (16-ounce) bag shred-
   ded Brussels sprouts

It's the cheesy sprinkle topping that makes this salad so delectable. I make a huge batch of the topping and always have it in my house to use on popcorn and roasted vegetables. If you've never had it before, nutritional yeast has a cheesy flavor somewhat similar to Parmesan, is a great source of protein, and is loaded with B vitamins. It's easy to find in most grocery stores in the spice aisle. For other ways to use it, check out the vegan cheese sauce in One-Pot Vegan Mac and Cheese (page 97).

1. **To make the vinaigrette:** In a small bowl, whisk together the lemon juice, mustard, and olive oil. Season with salt and pepper to taste. Or combine the ingredients in a jar and shake vigorously. Set aside.

2. **To make the cheesy sprinkle topping:** In a food processor, combine the almonds, cashews, nutritional yeast, salt, and garlic powder, and pulse until the mixture resembles large grains of sand. Set aside.

3. **To make the salad:** In a large mixing bowl, combine the kale and olive oil and massage gently with your hands for about 2 minutes, until the kale has softened. Add the shredded Brussels sprouts. Toss with the vinaigrette, and sprinkle with the cheesy sprinkle topping.

QUICK TIP: Sub in freshly grated Parmesan cheese for the nutty topping, if desired.

INGREDIENT TIP: Find shredded Brussels sprouts in the produce aisle or shred them yourself using the shredder attachment of the food processor. You will need about 2 large lemons to yield ¼ cup of juice, or use bottled lemon juice.

VEGETARIAN TACO SALAD

PREP TIME: **20 MINUTES**

NO COOK, NUT-FREE, QUICK

SERVES 4

For the avocado sour cream

2 avocados

½ cup sour cream

Juice of 1 lime

For the taco salad

6 cups chopped
   romaine lettuce

1 (15.5-ounce) can
   black beans, drained
   and rinsed

2 cups canned
   corn, drained

2 cups shredded ched-
   dar cheese

1 cup diced scallions,
   green and white parts

1 cup diced red
   bell pepper

Tortilla strips or crum-
   bled tortilla chips

1 cup pico de gallo

Ranch dressing, or other
   dressing of your choice

Are you one of those people (like me) who prefers a taco salad to a big cheesy plate of enchiladas? Then this is the meal for you. You'll leave the table with a spring in your step because although this salad is filling, it won't weigh you down. A taco salad is versatile in that you can replace or add ingredients customized to your moods and cravings. Add sliced jalapeños for a spicy kick, or toss in some Cauliflower and Walnut "Meat" Crumbles (page 64) for a meaty alternative.

1. **To make the avocado sour cream:** In a food processor, combine the avocados, sour cream, and lime juice, and pulse until blended. Set it aside.

2. **To make the salad:** Divide the lettuce among 4 bowls. Add the black beans, corn, cheese, scallions, bell pepper, and tortilla strips in piles on top of the lettuce on each plate. Add pico de gallo and a dollop of the avocado sour cream to the top of each salad.

3. Top with tortilla strips, drizzle with ranch dressing to taste, and serve immediately.

QUICK TIP: You can make the avocado sour cream ahead of time and store it in an airtight container for up to four days.

VARIATION TIP: Cube a package of extra-firm tofu and/or two sweet potatoes, and toss with taco seasoning. In a saucepan, sauté them in olive oil over medium-high heat for 10 minutes, and add one or both to the salad for a filling punch of protein and nutrients.

Lentil Shepherd's Pie, page 82

CHAPTER FIVE

Hearty Mains

◇

CAULIFLOWER AND WALNUT "MEAT" CRUMBLES

PREP TIME: 5 MINUTES **COOK TIME: 20 MINUTES**

DAIRY-FREE, GLUTEN-FREE, OFF THE SHELF, QUICK, VEGAN

SERVES 4

1 (10-ounce) bag frozen riced cauli-flower, thawed

1 cup finely chopped walnuts

2 garlic cloves, minced

1 teaspoon chili powder

1 teaspoon ground cumin

1 teaspoon dried oregano

1 teaspoon onion powder

1 teaspoon sea salt

1 teaspoon freshly ground black pepper

VARIATION TIP: *Make "cheesy" crumbles by adding a tablespoon of nutritional yeast to the mixing bowl.*

This is my preferred meat substitute for everything from chili to casseroles to salads. The textures are similar, but the nutrition profile is not. Here you get the fiber and B vitamins from the cauliflower and the protein and good fats from the walnuts. Take that, meat! Add it to the Vegetarian Taco Salad (page 60) or to the Baked Cheesy Zucchini Boats (page 65), or simply fold it into tortillas for Taco Tuesday—don't forget all the fixings!

1. Preheat the oven to 350°F. Line a large baking sheet with parchment paper.

2. In a large mixing bowl, combine the thawed riced cauliflower, walnuts, garlic, chili powder, cumin, oregano, onion powder, salt, and pepper, and stir well.

3. Spread the cauliflower mixture on the baking sheet using a spatula or wooden spoon to create a single layer.

4. Bake the mixture for 10 minutes, stir, then bake an additional 10 minutes, until the combination is golden brown, but not burnt.

BAKED CHEESY ZUCCHINI BOATS

PREP TIME: **10 MINUTES**   COOK TIME: **30 MINUTES**

5-INGREDIENT, ONE POT

SERVES 4

4 medium zucchini

2 tablespoons extra-virgin olive oil, for drizzling

Salt

Freshly ground black pepper

2 (15-ounce) cans cooked lentils, drained and rinsed

2 cups diced tomatoes

1 cup shredded cheddar cheese

VARIATION TIP: *This is a basic recipe for a reason. It means that the variations are limited only by your imagination. Take it south of the border by adding corn and tortilla strips, and garnish with salsa; give it an Italian flair by using shredded mozzarella and topping with marinara sauce; or hit the Greek islands with black olives, feta, and a dollop of Greek yogurt. There is a world of options.*

This has been a favorite recipe of mine for many years. And it lends itself to so many variations, like using black beans instead of the lentils, or using the Cauliflower and Walnut "Meat" Crumbles (page 64) as the filler. It's a very basic recipe: Zucchini + beans + veggies + cheese + sauce (if desired) but so good that you may find it making a frequent appearance in your weekly meal rotation, though never exactly with the same ingredient combo.

1. Preheat the oven to 400°F and line a baking sheet with parchment paper.

2. Cut the zucchini in half lengthwise. Using a spoon, gently scrape out some of the insides, enough to create a "boat." Place the zucchinis cut-side up on the prepared baking sheet. Drizzle lightly with the olive oil, and sprinkle with salt and pepper to taste.

3. Bake the zucchini for 20 minutes, or until the edges start to turn brown, then remove from the oven. Divide the lentils among the zucchini boats and bake another 5 minutes until heated through. Remove from the oven, set an oven rack 3 to 4 inches from the broiler, and turn the oven to broil.

4. Top each boat with diced tomatoes and cheese. Place them under the broiler for 2 to 3 minutes, until the cheese is melted. Serve immediately.

ROASTED PECAN-CRUSTED BUTTERNUT SQUASH STEAKS

PREP TIME: 10 MINUTES   **COOK TIME: 25 MINUTES**

5-INGREDIENT, GLUTEN-FREE

SERVES 4

1 butternut squash (see Ingredient Tip)

2 tablespoons olive oil, for brushing

Salt

Freshly ground black pepper

8 tablespoons (1 stick) unsalted butter

½ cup maple syrup

1 cup chopped pecans

INGREDIENT TIP: *Choose a butternut squash with as long as neck as possible because the steaks are cut out of the neck. Seed, bake, peel, and cube the remaining butternut squash, toss in taco seasoning, and use on the Vegetarian Taco Salad (page 60).*

You might have heard of cauliflower steaks, but here is something even better: butternut squash steaks. Before you peel the squash, pop it into the microwave for about 30 seconds. It makes peeling it so much easier.

1. Preheat the oven to 400°F. Line a baking sheet with parchment paper.

2. Cut the neck off the squash and reserve the base for another use. Put the neck in the microwave for 30 seconds, then peel the skin off the squash. (You may need to use a knife if the peel is resistant).

3. Cut the squash into ¾-inch-thick "steaks." Lay them on the baking sheet and brush or spray both sides with olive oil. Sprinkle with salt and pepper to taste, and put them in the oven.

4. Bake for 20 minutes, flipping halfway through.

5. In a small bowl, heat the butter in the microwave in 10-second increments until melted. Stir in the maple syrup and pecans.

6. Remove the squash steaks from the oven, drizzle the steaks generously with the butter mixture, then return the steaks to the oven. Bake for an additional 5 minutes, until the squash steaks are lightly golden.

BARBECUE TOFU RICE BOWLS

PREP TIME: **10 MINUTES**   COOK TIME: **20 MINUTES**

NUT-FREE, QUICK

SERVES 4

2 (14-ounce) blocks extra-firm tofu, drained

½ cup barbecue sauce, plus additional for drizzling

2 cups uncooked brown instant rice

2 (15-ounce) cans yellow corn, drained

1 cup shredded cheddar cheese

2 avocados, peeled, pitted, and sliced

2 tablespoons minced fresh cilantro

INGREDIENT TIP: *To make crispy tofu, wrap the tofu in a tea towel and place it on a large plate. Top the tofu with another plate and a heavy (preferably cast iron) pan. Let it sit for 25 minutes until most of the liquid is drained from the tofu.*

Tofu is a great source of protein and is a perfect chameleon because it takes on the flavor of whatever you cook it in. If you have a soy allergy, you can substitute black beans in place of the tofu; just toss the black beans with the barbecue sauce and bake for 10 minutes.

1. Preheat the oven to 400°F and line a baking sheet with parchment paper.

2. Wrap the tofu in a clean tea towel or paper towels and gently press out as much liquid as possible.

3. Transfer the tofu to a cutting board and cut into ½-inch cubes. In a mixing bowl, combine the tofu cubes and barbecue sauce, tossing gently until the tofu is fully covered.

4. Arrange the tofu in a single layer on the prepared baking sheet. Bake for 20 minutes, shaking the pan about halfway through.

5. As the tofu cooks, prepare the rice according to package directions.

6. Divide the rice among 4 serving bowls, and add the corn, cheese, and avocado in piles over the rice. Add the tofu cubes to each bowl, and sprinkle with minced cilantro. Add a drizzle of barbecue sauce just before serving.

MAKE IT VEGAN: Substitute the cheese with a nondairy version, leave it off altogether, or replace the cheese with sliced tomatoes or black olives.

EASY BRUSSELS-SPROUTS VEGGIE BURGERS

PREP TIME: **10 MINUTES**   COOK TIME: **16 MINUTES**

NUT-FREE, QUICK

SERVES 4

For the cheesy mayo buns (optional)

½ cup shredded cheddar cheese

¼ cup mayonnaise

½ teaspoon onion powder

4 hamburger buns

For the patties

1 pound Brussels sprouts, trimmed

1 cup grated Parmesan cheese

¼ cup almond flour

3 tablespoons chopped scallions, green parts only

2 large eggs

1 cup soft goat cheese

1 tablespoon olive oil

I consider myself to be somewhat of a veggie-burger queen. My obsession for veggie burgers is no secret to anyone who knows me. I have written and read countless articles about veggie burgers, ranging from recipes to finding and rating the best veggie burgers in town. The varieties are endless; veggie burgers can be made from so many things: mushrooms, beets, black beans, or tofu. This is one of my favorite veggie-burger recipes, and your guests won't know there are Brussels sprouts in this recipe unless you tell them. Gluten-free? Toss the buns and serve with Roasted Garlic–Parmesan Carrot Fries (page 34) instead.

1. **To make the cheesy mayo buns (if using):** Preheat the oven to 350°F. Line a baking sheet with parchment paper.

2. In a mixing bowl, combine the cheese, mayonnaise, and onion powder, and mix together. Divide the mayo mixture among 4 hamburger buns, place them open-faced on the baking sheet, and bake for 10 minutes, until toasty (take care that they don't burn). Put the buns on plates and set aside.

3. **To make the patties:** Using the shredder attachment on the food processor, shred the Brussels sprouts. Transfer the shredded sprouts to a large mixing bowl, add the grated Parmesan cheese and almond flour, and mix well. Add the scallions, eggs, and goat cheese, and use your hands to combine.

4. In a large skillet, heat the oil over medium-high heat. Form the Brussels-sprout mixture into four patties. Cook the patties for 6 minutes, flipping after 3 minutes. They should be firm and lightly browned.

5. Remove them from the pan and let the patties rest on a paper towel–lined plate for 30 seconds. Top the cheesy buns with the veggie patties and enjoy.

QUICK TIP: Most grocery stores sell shredded Brussels sprouts, which is an excellent time-saver. Usually, they're found in the produce aisle near the bags of lettuce and other chopped vegetables.

ONE-POT RICE AND BEAN CASSEROLE

PREP TIME: **10 MINUTES**   COOK TIME: **20 MINUTES**

NUT-FREE, ONE POT, QUICK

SERVES 4

1 tablespoon olive oil

1 large white onion, diced

1 large green bell pepper, diced

3 scallions, white and green parts, chopped

1 tablespoon taco seasoning

1½ cups uncooked instant brown rice

3 cups vegetable broth

1 (15-ounce) can black beans, drained and rinsed

1 (8-ounce) can tomato sauce

½ cup salsa or enchilada sauce

1 cup shredded cheddar or jack cheese

There's nothing better than a one-pot meal, especially if it's your turn to clean the dishes. This casserole lifts simple rice and beans to new heights. You can serve this as a main dish or use it as a filling for tacos. I like this dish with tortilla chips, sour cream, and diced tomatoes. Some sliced avocado gives it even more of a lift.

1. In a large pot, heat the olive oil over medium-high heat. Add the onion, green pepper, and scallions, and stir. Add the taco seasoning and continue to cook until the vegetables soften, about 5 minutes.

2. Add the uncooked rice and stir, then add the vegetable broth. Bring to a boil, cover, and reduce the heat to low. Let it simmer for 5 minutes, until most of the liquid is absorbed by the rice. Add the black beans, tomato sauce, and salsa. Stir the rice mixture and raise the heat to medium. Let it cook an additional 5 minutes, or until heated thoroughly, stirring occasionally.

3. Add the shredded cheese to the rice mixture, and stir until the cheese is melted, about 3 minutes. Serve immediately.

QUICK TIP: You can save time by using pre-cooked rice. Just omit the vegetable broth and skip the first part of step 2.

VARIATION TIP: Feeling a little extra? Try doubling the cheese or adding avocado slices at the end.

CURRIED LENTILS WITH KALE

PREP TIME: 5 MINUTES   **COOK TIME: 21 MINUTES**

DAIRY-FREE, GLUTEN-FREE, ONE POT, QUICK, VEGAN

SERVES 4

2 tablespoons olive oil

1 medium onion, diced

½ teaspoon salt

1 cup chopped walnuts

2 cups canned lentils, drained

1 tablespoon curry powder

½ cup full-fat coconut milk (see Ingredient Tip)

4 cups chopped curly kale, rinsed, ribs removed

4 cups cooked rice, for serving (optional)

INGREDIENT TIP: *Don't use the cartons of coconut milk you find in the dairy section. Instead, buy the full-fat canned coconut milk found in the international aisle. It's thicker and better for cooking.*

Did you know that the largest producer and exporter of lentils in the world is Canada? These protein and nutrient beasts are combined here with heart-healthy, brain-boosting walnuts to create a rich meal with just the right amount of crunch. This is best served over rice or farro, another whole grain that's easy to cook. You can also easily add peas and carrots to the mix for some color and even more nutrients.

1. In a large skillet, heat the olive oil over medium-high heat. Add the onions and salt, and cook for 5 minutes, stirring often, until the onions have softened.

2. Add the walnuts and cook another 3 minutes, until fragrant. Add the lentils and curry powder, and stir well. Let them cook about 3 minutes.

3. Add the coconut milk and kale. Let the mixture simmer for about 10 minutes, stirring occasionally, until the kale has wilted and reduced. Serve immediately over rice, if using.

SWEET POTATO AND BLACK BEAN FRITTERS

PREP TIME: **15 MINUTES**   COOK TIME: **15 MINUTES**

DAIRY-FREE, GLUTEN-FREE, NUT-FREE, QUICK, VEGAN

SERVES 4

2 large sweet potatoes

1 (15-ounce) can black
   beans, drained
   and rinsed

1 cup cooked quinoa
   (see Ingredient Tip)

½ cup diced white onion

¼ cup chopped
   fresh parsley

2 tablespoons
   ground cumin

½ teaspoon paprika

1 teaspoon garlic powder

Salt

2 tablespoons olive oil

INGREDIENT TIP: *Cooked
quinoa can be found in the
international aisle of your
local grocery store, usually
in pouches. Or, you can
swap out the quinoa for
cooked rice or farro.*

Sweet potatoes and black beans are the perfect duo in vegetarian cooking. They create such a lovely texture, a balanced taste, and a health boost that is off the charts. This combo makes excellent veggie burgers, taco fillings and, here, patties. These are not deep-fried like traditional fritters, so feel free to eat them to your heart's (and stomach's) content.

1. Pierce the potatoes a few times with a fork and place them on a microwave-safe plate. Microwave on high for 5 minutes, flipping halfway through, until the potatoes are tender. Remove them from the microwave and (carefully, to avoid escaping steam) slice each potato in half lengthwise to speed cooling. Let the potatoes cool about 5 minutes.

2. When the potatoes have cooled enough to handle, scoop out the flesh into a medium mixing bowl. Add the black beans. Using a potato masher, mash the sweet potatoes and black beans until they are smooth but still slightly chunky.

3. Add the cooked quinoa, onions, parsley, cumin, paprika, garlic powder, and salt to taste, to the mixing bowl with the sweet potato and black beans. Using your hands or a spoon, mix the ingredients together.

4. In a large skillet, heat the olive oil over medium-high heat. Using about ¼ cup of sweet potato mixture, form small patties that are about 1 inch thick. Working in batches if necessary, place the fritters into the heated skillet and cook for 8 minutes, flipping each one halfway through.

5. As the fritters cook, line a large dinner plate with two layers of paper towels. As you remove each cooked patty from the pan, place it on the paper towels to soak up excess oil. Serve immediately.

DOUBLE DECKER BROCCOLI TACOS

NUT-FREE, QUICK

SERVES 4

1 tablespoon olive oil

2 shallots, diced

2 (10-ounce) packages frozen riced broccoli (see Ingredient Tip)

1 (15-ounce) can black beans, drained and rinsed

1 cup store-bought hummus

1 tablespoon white wine vinegar

8 (7- to 8-inch) flour tortillas

8 hard taco shells

1 cup diced tomatoes

1 cup shredded cheddar cheese

INGREDIENT TIP: *If you can't find riced broccoli at your grocery store, you can rice a head of broccoli using the food processor. Just use the shredder attachment and shred the broccoli so it resembles rice. Be careful not to overprocess and liquify the broccoli. One large head of broccoli should yield about 2 cups of riced broccoli.*

The No. 7 Restaurant in Brooklyn has a cult following, for good reason. I loved to swing by to get their double decker broccoli tacos, in particular. I've re-created it here, and it's darn delicious (if I may say so myself), but my recipe will never measure up to the genius of the original. It's a must-try for any vegetarian in New York.

1. In a large skillet, heat the olive oil over medium-high heat. Add the shallots and cook for about 3 minutes to soften, stirring occasionally.

2. Add the riced broccoli and cook 10 to 15 minutes, until the broccoli is heated through, stirring occasionally.

3. As the broccoli cooks, in a food processor, combine the black beans, hummus, and white wine vinegar, and pulse until well blended.

4. Wrap the flour tortillas in a damp paper towel and microwave for 20 seconds.

5. Spread 1 to 2 tablespoons of the black bean and hummus mixture on each of the flour tortillas. Place a hard taco shell in the middle of each tortilla and wrap the tortilla up around each shell.

6. Spoon the riced broccoli mixture into the hard taco shells. Top with diced tomatoes and cheese, and serve immediately.

ONE-POT VEGAN JAMBALAYA

PREP TIME: **5 MINUTES**   COOK TIME: **20 MINUTES**

DAIRY-FREE, NUT-FREE, ONE POT, QUICK, VEGAN

SERVES 6

2 tablespoons olive oil

1 large white
  onion, diced

1 green bell
  pepper, diced

2 celery stalks, diced

1 garlic clove, minced

1 tablespoon
  onion powder

1 tablespoon dried basil

2 teaspoons
  smoked paprika

1 teaspoon salt

2 cups uncooked instant
  brown rice

4 cups vegetable broth
  or water

2 (15-ounce) cans red
  kidney beans, drained
  and rinsed

Creole and New Orleans cooking basically all starts with one thing: the Holy Trinity: equal parts onions, peppers, and celery. This is an auspicious start to a cuisine known for its comforting, spicy, smoky nature. You can't have your beignets until you finish your dinner, and with this vegan jambalaya, that will be easy to do.

1. In a large, deep pot, heat the olive oil over medium-high heat. Add the onion, green pepper, and celery, and stir. Add the garlic, onion powder, basil, paprika, and salt. Cook for 5 to 7 minutes, until the vegetables have softened.

2. Add the rice and the vegetable broth, and bring to a boil. Cover and reduce heat to low. Let it simmer for 5 minutes, until most of the broth is absorbed.

3. Add the kidney beans and mix well. Continue to cook, covered, another 5 minutes, until the beans are heated thoroughly. Serve warm.

EGGPLANT PARMESAN BAKE

PREP TIME: **10 MINUTES**   COOK TIME: **35 MINUTES**

5-INGREDIENT, NUT-FREE

SERVES 6

3 small eggplants

¼ cup extra-virgin
olive oil

½ teaspoon salt

8 tablespoons
(1 stick) unsalted
butter, melted

1 cup Italian-seasoned
dry bread crumbs

1½ cups grated Parme-
san cheese, divided

1 (24-ounce) jar mari-
nara sauce, divided

QUICK TIP: *This dish is
equally delicious with broccoli and cauliflower in place
of the eggplant.*

Eggplant Parmesan is such a popular dish in Italian
American cooking. However, eggplant can be a little
difficult—do you salt it? For how long? Today's varieties of eggplants do not need to be salted to remove the
bitter flavor. I like to use three smaller eggplants instead
of one large one because I find smaller ones tend to be
naturally sweeter.

1. Preheat the oven to 375°F.

2. In a 9-by-13-inch baking dish, layer the pieces of eggplant, drizzle with the olive oil, and sprinkle with salt.
   Roast in the oven for 10 minutes.

3. While the eggplant roasts, in a mixing bowl, combine
   the melted butter, bread crumbs, and ½ cup of the
   grated cheese. Set aside.

4. Pour half of the marinara sauce over the eggplant and
   wrap the baking dish tightly with aluminum foil. Bake
   for an additional 15 minutes. Remove the foil, add the
   remaining marinara sauce, and sprinkle with remaining
   1 cup of cheese. Re-cover with aluminum foil and bake
   an additional 5 minutes.

5. Remove the dish from the oven, take off the foil, and
   cover the eggplant bake with the bread crumb mixture.
   Place it back in the oven for an additional 3 minutes,
   until the bread crumbs are golden brown.

CREAMY MUSHROOM QUINOTTO

NUT-FREE, QUICK

SERVES 4

For the quinoa

1 tablespoon olive oil

1 cup uncooked
quinoa, rinsed

1¾ cups vegetable broth
or water

For the mushrooms

1 tablespoon butter

2 minced shallots

1 (16-ounce) package
sliced mushrooms

½ teaspoon dried thyme

½ teaspoon
dried oregano

¼ cup vegetable broth
or water

½ cup half-and-half

¼ cup shredded Parme-
san cheese

MAKE IT VEGAN: *Substi-
tute coconut milk for the
half-and-half, olive oil for
the butter, and nutritional
yeast for the cheese.*

Quinotto is quinoa prepared like a risotto, hence
the hybrid name. If you have ever made risotto from
arborio rice, you know how time-consuming it can
be. Although I don't have the patience for traditional
risotto, I do have cravings for a creamy grain. Voilà!—
quinotto, a creamy, dreamy dish without the extra time.

1. **To make the quinoa:** In a medium saucepan, heat
the olive oil over medium-high heat. Add the quinoa
and stir briskly for 1 minute, then add the vegetable
broth. Cover the pot and reduce the heat to low. Let
the quinoa simmer for 15 minutes, or until the liquid
is absorbed.

2. **To make the mushrooms:** In a large skillet, heat
the butter over medium heat. Add the minced shallots,
mushrooms, thyme, and oregano to the skillet and stir.
Let them cook about 3 minutes, until the mushrooms
begin to show signs of shrinking.

3. Add the vegetable broth to the skillet and stir to
deglaze the pan, not allowing any mushrooms to stick.
Simmer until the broth is mostly evaporated, about
4 minutes. Add the half-and-half and Parmesan to the
skillet, then stir to mix well.

4. Fold the quinoa into the mushroom mixture. Simmer
until the sauce thickens slightly, about 3 minutes, then
turn off the heat. Allow the dish to sit for 2 minutes
before serving.

CARROT AND WHITE-BEAN VEGGIE BURGER

PREP TIME: **10 MINUTES**   COOK TIME: **10 MINUTES**

DAIRY-FREE, NUT-FREE, QUICK

SERVES 4

2 cups shredded carrots

½ cup cooked quinoa

1 small yellow onion, minced

1 tablespoon cornmeal

2 tablespoons all-purpose flour

¼ cup minced fresh parsley

¼ teaspoon salt

1 (15-ounce) can cannellini beans, drained and rinsed

1 large egg

1 tablespoon olive oil

Rolls, for serving (optional)

Lettuce, for serving (optional)

Tomato slices, for serving (optional)

QUICK TIP: *Buy the carrots pre-shredded and the onions and parsley pre-chopped to save yourself some prep time.*

Once you get the hang of making a recipe like this, you will begin to learn how to mix and match ingredients to make a veggie burger all your own. Sub in beets for carrots, for instance, or basil for parsley. The options are endless, and the more you experiment, the more you will learn what works. I love cooking up a veggie burger, then crumbling it into a pasta sauce or sprinkling on top of a salad to boost the protein and veggie content of a dish. To make this burger extra delicious, top it with the sweet-potato mustard from the Carrot Slaw Dogs with Sweet-Potato Mustard (page 44). Keep it gluten-free, or serve it on a bun with all the fixings.

1. In a large mixing bowl, toss the carrots, quinoa, onion, cornmeal, flour, parsley, salt, cannellini beans, and egg, using your hands or a spoon to mix well.

2. In a large skillet, heat the oil over medium-high heat. Shape the mixture into four 1½-inch-thick patties. Place them in the skillet, cooking them for 5 minutes on each side. Remove them from the skillet and let them sit for 2 minutes on a paper towel–lined plate.

3. Serve alone or on rolls with lettuce, tomato, or any burger toppings of your choice.

MASHED-BEAN QUESADILLA

PREP TIME: 10 MINUTES   **COOK TIME: 20 MINUTES**

SERVES 4

12 (7- to 8-inch) flour tortillas

1 tablespoon olive oil

1 large white onion, diced

Salt

2 (15-ounce) cans black beans, drained and rinsed

2 tablespoons unsalted butter

2 cups diced tomatoes

2 cups shredded cheddar cheese

Olive oil cooking spray

MAKE IT GLUTEN-FREE:
Substitute the flour tortillas with soft corn tortillas.

Did you know that *quesadilla* literally means "little cheesy thing"? I challenge you to find someone who doesn't love little cheesy things. For this take on the classic Mexican dish, I love to mash black beans with butter; it's a quick way to replicate the texture of refried beans while adding a little creaminess and flavor. Then top with cheddar to give it a quesadilla cheesiness worthy of its name.

1. Preheat the oven to 350°F. Line a large baking sheet with parchment paper and lay half of the tortillas down in a single layer. You may need to use 2 baking sheets.

2. In a medium-size pot, heat the oil over medium-high heat. Add the onion and salt to taste. Cook until almost translucent, about 3 minutes. Add the beans and stir until heated through, about 5 minutes. Remove from the heat and add the butter. Mash the beans with a potato masher. Divide the bean mash among the six tortillas. Top with diced tomatoes and cheese.

3. Top the tortillas and toppings with the remaining 6 tortillas. Spray lightly with olive oil. Bake for 10 minutes, until the quesadillas are golden brown. Remove and cut each quesadilla in half before serving. They're delicious served with sour cream, salsa, and/or guacamole.

PINEAPPLE-CASHEW STIR-FRY

PREP TIME: **5 MINUTES**   COOK TIME: **20 MINUTES**

5-INGREDIENT, OFF THE SHELF, ONE POT, QUICK, VEGAN

SERVES 4

2 tablespoons olive oil

1 (16-ounce) bag frozen
  stir-fry vegetables

3 tablespoons soy sauce

1 cup raw
  unsalted cashews

1 (8-ounce) can diced
  pineapple, undrained

2 cups cooked rice

MAKE IT GLUTEN-FREE:
*You can replace the soy
sauce with liquid aminos.
Liquid aminos are nat-
urally gluten-free and
taste exactly like their soy
counterpart. You can find
them in the aisle with the
vinegar or by the soy sauce,
depending on how your
store categorizes it.*

The combination of tangy pineapple with mellow, nutty cashews is irresistible, which is why this recipe is one of my very favorite easy weeknight meals. I always keep a few cans of diced pineapple in my pantry for this recipe, but the ingredient also works perfectly as an addition to smoothies or over yogurt in the morning.

1. In a large skillet, heat the oil over medium-high heat. Add the frozen vegetables and stir. Let them cook for 15 minutes, until the vegetables are no longer frozen through, stirring occasionally. Add the soy sauce, cashews, and undrained pineapple with its juices. Cook an additional 5 minutes, until heated through.

2. Divide the rice over 4 serving plates and top with the pineapple-and-cashew stir-fry.

ROASTED POTATO AND TOMATO CASSEROLE

PREP TIME: 20 MINUTES   **COOK TIME: 35 MINUTES**

SERVES 6

1 sweet potato, cut into ½-inch pieces

1 white potato, cut into ½-inch pieces

2 carrots, cut into ½-inch pieces

4 tablespoons olive oil, divided, plus more for drizzling

Salt

Freshly ground black pepper

1 white onion, cut into thin rings

1 orange or red bell pepper, chopped into ½-inch pieces

1 zucchini, peeled and cut into ½-inch pieces

1 yellow squash, peeled and cut into ½-inch pieces

2 to 3 large red vine tomatoes, sliced

½ cup grated Parmesan cheese

2 tablespoons bread crumbs

I make this once a week. It's the kind of dish every vegetable lover dreams of. Don't be daunted by the amount of prep required here because once the prep is finished, the recipe is basically hands-off. Be sure not to over-oil the vegetables; not every surface of every vegetable must be coated with oil. You want to taste the vegetables in the end, not the oil.

1. Preheat the oven to 400°F. In a 9-by-13-inch baking dish, toss the sweet potato, white potato, and carrots with 2 tablespoons of the olive oil, and salt and pepper to taste, until the potatoes are evenly coated. Spread the potatoes and carrots evenly in the dish.

2. Place the onion slices evenly atop the potato mixture, followed by the bell pepper, zucchini, and squash. Drizzle with 1 tablespoon of olive oil.

3. Place the tomato slices over the zucchini and squash. Drizzle with the remaining 1 tablespoon of olive oil. Bake for 30 minutes.

4. In a small bowl, combine the grated Parmesan cheese and the bread crumbs. After the casserole has cooked for 30 minutes, remove it from the oven and sprinkle it with the bread crumb mixture. Lightly drizzle with olive oil, and cook for an additional 5 minutes, until the bread crumbs are golden brown. Serve warm.

LENTIL SHEPHERD'S PIE

PREP TIME: **10 MINUTES**   COOK TIME: **45 MINUTES**

DAIRY-FREE, GLUTEN-FREE, NUT-FREE, OFF THE SHELF, VEGAN

SERVES 4

1 (16-ounce) package frozen cauliflower florets

3 cups vegetable broth, divided

Salt

Freshly ground black pepper

1 (15-ounce) can cooked lentils

1 (16-ounce) package frozen peas and carrots

1 medium white onion, diced

1 garlic clove, minced

1 (6-ounce) can tomato paste

VARIATION TIP: *Replace the lentils with the Cauliflower and Walnut "Meat" Crumbles on (page 64) or crumble the Carrot and White-Bean Veggie Burgers on (page 78).*

Traditional shepherd's pie is a ground-meat pie topped with mashed potatoes, a favorite in the UK. Here's a lighter, healthier veggie take. The lentils have just the right amount of flavor and texture that they perfectly replace the meat. And this mashed cauliflower is just as delicious as mashed potatoes. It's so good, in fact, that you can also use this mashed cauliflower as a side for the Roasted Pecan-Crusted Butternut Squash Steaks (page 66) or Sweet Potato and Black Bean Fritters (page 72).

1. In a medium saucepan, combine the cauliflower and 2 cups of vegetable broth, and bring to a boil over high heat. Reduce the heat and let it simmer for 20 minutes, until the cauliflower is tender.

2. Drain the cauliflower and add it back to the pot. Mash it with a potato masher until the cauliflower is a mashed-potato consistency. Season with salt and pepper.

3. Preheat the oven to 375°F. In a 3-quart baking dish, combine the lentils, peas and carrots, onion, garlic, remaining 1 cup vegetable broth, and tomato paste. Add salt and pepper to taste. Stir until well combined. Bake for 15 minutes, until peas and carrots are heated through.

4. Remove from the oven and spread the mashed cauliflower over the lentil mixture. Sprinkle with salt and pepper. Bake for an additional 5 minutes, until the cauliflower begins to brown slightly. Serve hot.

Brown-Butter Mushroom Ravioli, page 94

CHAPTER SIX

Pasta and Noodles

5-INGREDIENT ROLLED SPINACH LASAGNA

PREP TIME: **10 MINUTES**   COOK TIME: **40 MINUTES**

5-INGREDIENT, NUT-FREE

SERVES 4

12 lasagna noodles

1 (15-ounce) container whole-milk ricotta cheese

1 (10-ounce) package frozen spinach, thawed and squeezed dry

Salt

Freshly ground black pepper

1 (24-ounce) jar marinara sauce, divided

1 cup shredded mozzarella cheese

If you've never had rolled lasagna, you're in for a treat. Basically, you take flat lasagna noodles, and roll them around a filling. It's portable and a crowd-pleaser, so it's my go-to recipe anytime I need to bake a dish for an event. It's also incredibly versatile; you can add whatever you have on hand, whether you want to sauté diced onions and green peppers to add to the ricotta mixture or supplement it with the Cauliflower and Walnut "Meat" Crumbles (page 64).

1. Preheat the oven to 425°F. Line a baking sheet with parchment paper.

2. Cook the lasagna noodles in boiling, salted water until just a little firmer than al dente, about 10 minutes. Carefully remove them from the water and lay them in a single layer on the baking sheet.

3. In a mixing bowl, combine the ricotta and spinach, and add salt and pepper to taste.

4. Pour 1 cup of the marinara sauce into a 9-by-13-inch baking dish.

5. Spread the ricotta mixture evenly on each lasagna noodle and carefully roll each noodle up into a jelly roll. Place each lasagna roll seam-side down in the baking dish with the marinara sauce. Pour the remaining marinara sauce over the lasagna rolls. Cover the dish tightly with aluminum foil and bake for 20 minutes.

6. Carefully remove the foil and sprinkle the cheese on top of the lasagna rolls. Bake uncovered for an additional 10 minutes or until the cheese is golden and the marinara sauce is bubbling.

AVOCADO AND LEMON PASTA

PREP TIME: **10 MINUTES**   COOK TIME: **10 MINUTES**

NUT-FREE, QUICK

SERVES 4

12 ounces uncooked linguine

2 large ripe avocados, peeled and pitted

¼ cup plain Greek yogurt

Juice of 1 lemon

1 tablespoon extra-virgin olive oil

¼ cup fresh basil leaves, roughly chopped

Water, as needed

Salt

Freshly ground black pepper

Zest of 1 lemon

VARIATION TIP: *To add a little extra flair, slice a pint of cherry tomatoes in half and place them on a foil-lined baking sheet. Lightly drizzle with olive oil, then place under the broiler for 3 to 5 minutes, until the tomatoes are slightly charred. Serve on top of the avocado pasta.*

For a light and refreshing twist on spaghetti and marinara, try this tangy, creamy, healthy pasta dish, perfect for when the weather gets a little warmer. I like to add broiled cherry tomatoes (see Variation Tip) and sliced almonds to make this dish even heartier.

1. Cook the pasta in salted boiling water until al dente, about 10 minutes.

2. Meanwhile, make the sauce. In a food processor, scoop out the flesh of the avocados. Add the yogurt, lemon juice, olive oil, and basil. Pulse until well blended. If the sauce is too thick, add 1 tablespoon of water, and pulse. Continue to add water, 1 tablespoon at a time, until the sauce reaches the right consistency, thick but pourable. Add salt and pepper to taste.

3. Drain the pasta and return it to the pot. Add the avocado sauce and mix with the pasta until the noodles are coated. Plate the pasta and top with lemon zest.

ONE-POT SPICY CURRY NOODLES

PREP TIME: 25 MINUTES   **COOK TIME: 20 MINUTES**

DAIRY-FREE, ONE POT, VEGAN

SERVES 4

1 (16-ounce) package thin rice noodles

2 tablespoons olive oil, divided

2 cups chopped frozen broccoli

2 garlic cloves, minced

2 tablespoons red curry paste (see Ingredient Tip)

1 (14-ounce) can full-fat coconut milk

1 tablespoon soy sauce

Juice of 1 lime

½ cup vegetable broth

¼ cup sliced scallions, green parts only

INGREDIENT TIP: *In its most basic form, red curry paste is made from red chiles, garlic, lemongrass, and turmeric. It can be found in the international aisle of your grocery store. However, check the label to make sure you are not buying a brand that contains fish sauce or shrimp paste.*

Canned full-fat coconut milk, rather than the cartons of coconut milk you buy in the refrigerated section of the grocery store, provides a thick, creamy base for use in cooking. This recipe is quicker than it looks at first glance. While the noodles soak, you can make practically the whole thing, so, in total it will take 25 to 30 minutes.

1. Soak the noodles in a bowl of warm water for 20 minutes.

2. While the noodles are soaking, in a large saucepan, heat 1 tablespoon of oil over medium-high heat. Add the broccoli and cook for 10 minutes, until the broccoli is softened. Remove and set aside.

3. In the same saucepan, heat the remaining 1 tablespoon oil over medium-high heat. Add the garlic and stir until softened and fragrant, about 2 minutes. Add the curry paste and stir until well mixed with the garlic. Add the coconut milk, soy sauce, and lime juice, and let simmer for 5 minutes.

4. Drain the noodles and add them to the saucepan with the coconut curry sauce. Stir to coat. Add half the vegetable broth, stir to combine, and let simmer about 3 minutes. Add the remaining vegetable broth and the broccoli. Stir and let simmer until the sauce has thickened slightly.

5. Serve immediately, topped with sliced scallions.

PASTA WITH WALNUT-CARROT PESTO

PREP TIME: **5 MINUTES**   COOK TIME: **10 MINUTES**

QUICK

SERVES 4

12 ounces uncooked spiral pasta

1 cup shredded carrots

½ cup lightly packed fresh basil leaves

1 garlic clove

⅓ cup chopped walnuts

½ cup grated Parmesan cheese

½ cup extra-virgin olive oil, plus more for drizzling

Salt

Freshly ground black pepper

I cannot get enough of pesto, especially when I make it with walnuts instead of (more traditional but pricier) pine nuts. Walnuts have a slight edge over pine nuts in the protein department and contain more healthy fats and potassium than most other nuts. I use this pesto as a base on pizzas as well. I just spread the pesto on store-bought pizza crust and add a light sprinkling of shredded Parmesan cheese before baking.

1. Cook the pasta in boiling, salted water until al dente, about 10 minutes.

2. In a food processor, combine the carrots, basil, garlic, walnuts, Parmesan, and olive oil. Add salt and pepper to taste. Pulse until combined; the pesto will be slightly chunky.

3. Drain the pasta and return it to the pot. Add the walnut-carrot pesto and stir to coat the noodles. Lightly drizzle the noodles with olive oil just before serving.

CREAMY CHEESY ASPARAGUS PASTA

PREP TIME: **5 MINUTES**   COOK TIME: **20 MINUTES**

NUT-FREE, QUICK

SERVES 4

12 ounces
  uncooked pasta

1 tablespoon olive oil

1 pound asparagus, cut
  into bite-sized pieces

2 shallots, minced

1 tablespoon
  unsalted butter

¼ teaspoon
  ground nutmeg

1 cup half-and-half

Salt

Freshly ground
  black pepper

1 cup shredded mozza-
  rella cheese

Nothing is better than a delectable sauce that you can sop up with a crusty bread. This simple pasta dish makes just that: a rich, creamy, smooth sauce that lends itself to licking the plate clean. Don't flat-out disregard the asparagus (because it is rich in fiber, antioxidants, and multiple other nutrients), but it can easily be traded for broccoli, cauliflower, carrots, or a combination of any of these vegetables. I throw in some Brussels sprouts to this recipe for extra nutrition.

1. Cook the pasta in boiling, salted water until al dente, according to package directions.

2. While the pasta is boiling, in a large saucepan, heat the oil over medium-high heat. Add the asparagus and shallots, and cook until softened, stirring frequently, about 10 minutes. Add the butter and nutmeg. Stir until the butter is melted, then add the half-and-half and salt and pepper to taste. Let the mixture simmer, about 5 minutes, until the sauce thickens slightly.

3. Drain the pasta, and add it to the saucepan with the creamy sauce. Stir to coat. Add the cheese, and stir until the cheese has melted, about 5 minutes. Serve immediately.

PESTO AND WHITE-BEAN PASTA

PREP TIME: **10 MINUTES**   COOK TIME: **10 MINUTES**

QUICK

SERVES 4

6 cups dried maca-
roni pasta

1 cup lightly packed
fresh basil leaves

2 tablespoons walnuts

¼ cup extra-virgin
olive oil

¼ cup grated Parmesan
cheese

1 (15.5-ounce) can white
cannellini beans,
drained and rinsed

I got the idea for this recipe from my Italian step-
mother, who was telling me about a dish she makes for
my very picky niece. Sneaking in beans and nuts is a
great way to hide some extra fiber and protein into a
very appealing pasta dish. The beans are pureed into the
pesto, making a creamy sauce.

1. Cook the pasta in salted, boiling water according to
   package directions until al dente.

2. While the pasta is cooking, combine the basil, walnuts, olive oil, Parmesan cheese, and beans in a food
   processor and process until smooth. Add 2 tablespoons
   of water at a time to thin the sauce out, if desired.

3. Drain the pasta and return to the cooking pot. Add the
   bean sauce and stir to combine well.

4. Serve immediately.

SPAGHETTI A LA LIMONE

PREP TIME: **5 MINUTES**   COOK TIME: **20 MINUTES**

5-INGREDIENT, NUT-FREE, QUICK

SERVES 4

12 ounces uncooked
 spaghetti

Juice of 4 lemons

½ cup grated Parme-
 san cheese

⅓ cup torn fresh basil
 leaves, divided

Zest of
 2 lemons, divided

Salt

Freshly ground
 black pepper

VARIATION TIP: *This is
an easy recipe to add the
broiled cherry tomatoes
from the tip in the recipe
for Avocado and Lemon
Pasta (page 88) or add
sautéed broccoli or Brussels
sprouts.*

Limone (Italian for "lemon") tastes tangy and fresh with
pasta. This is an excellent dish for those warm summer
nights when you are dining al fresco (Spanish, meaning
in the open air). Just make sure you don't confuse your
languages and ask to dine al fresco in Italy. In Italian,
the phrase means "in the cold" or, in some regions,
"in prison." You don't want to find yourself dining
behind bars!

1. Cook the pasta in boiling, salted water until firm,
   according to package directions. Drain the pasta,
   reserving 1 cup of pasta water.

2. Heat a large saucepan over medium-high heat. In the
   pan, combine the pasta, ¼ cup reserved pasta water,
   and lemon juice. Let the liquid simmer for about
   5 minutes, until most of the water has evaporated.

3. Add the Parmesan cheese, half of the basil leaves, and
   half of the lemon zest. Stir to combine. If the pasta is
   too dry, add ¼ cup of reserved pasta water at a time
   until the pasta is coated with the cheesy sauce. Divide
   among serving bowls and top with the remaining basil
   leaves and lemon zest.

BROWN-BUTTER MUSHROOM RAVIOLI

PREP TIME: **5 MINUTES**   COOK TIME: **15 MINUTES**

SERVES 4

1 (18-ounce) package ravioli, fresh or frozen

8 tablespoons (1 stick) unsalted butter

1 pound fancy/wild mushrooms (or button or cremini mushrooms)

½ cup chopped walnuts

½ cup shredded Parmesan cheese

2 tablespoons coarsely chopped fresh parsley

INGREDIENT TIPS: *Fancy and/or wild mushroom blends are often composed of a mixture of maitake, shiitake, oyster, and other varieties. It should be easy to find at the grocery store, but feel free to use regular button or cremini mushrooms as well. The recipe is delicious either way. You can use any ravioli of your choice; spinach ravioli or butternut squash ravioli both pair very well with the mushrooms and walnuts.*

When you cook butter for a few minutes, it turns brown and takes on a nutty aroma and flavor. It's a delicious topping not only for pasta, but also for vegetables and vegetable steaks like the Roasted Pecan-Crusted Butternut Squash Steaks (page 66). The key is to keep the butter moving once it starts to foam so it doesn't burn. If making the brown butter on its own, remove it just after it begins to foam and turn slightly brown.

1. Cook the ravioli in boiling, salted water until al dente, according to package directions. Drain and set aside.

2. Heat a large saucepan over medium-high heat. Add the butter and stir until the butter melts and begins to foam. Add the mushrooms and walnuts. Cook, stirring continuously, for 2 to 3 minutes until the mushrooms begin to shrink. Add the drained ravioli, and stir until coated.

3. Divide the ravioli and mushrooms onto serving plates. Sprinkle the plates evenly with the Parmesan cheese and fresh parsley.

4-INGREDIENT PUMPKIN PASTA

PREP TIME: 5 MINUTES   **COOK TIME: 20 MINUTES**

SERVES 4

12 ounces
uncooked pasta

1½ cups heavy cream

1 cup pure pumpkin
puree (not pumpkin
pie filling)

Salt

Freshly ground
black pepper

2 tablespoons chopped
fresh sage

To jump on the pumpkin-spice bandwagon, create this cozy, autumnal pasta dish and skip the expensive lattes. Your pumpkin spice will be more authentic anyway because it actually contains pumpkin; many "pumpkin spice" flavored items use a combination of cloves, nutmeg, and cinnamon, and skip the pumpkin altogether. This dish is best served with a side of warm, crusty bread and maybe some apple butter.

1. Cook the pasta in boiling, salted water until al dente, according to the package directions.

2. Meanwhile, in a large saucepan, heat the cream over medium-high heat. Stir for about 4 minutes, until the cream starts to reduce.

3. Add the pumpkin puree, and salt and pepper to taste. Stir, bring to a simmer, and let it cook for about 5 minutes. Add the sage and mix until well combined.

4. Drain the pasta and add it to the pumpkin sauce. Stir to coat. Serve immediately.

VEGETABLE, FETA, AND CASHEW PASTA SALAD

PREP TIME: **10 MINUTES**   COOK TIME: **10 MINUTES**

SERVES 6

4 cups uncooked
   spiral pasta

2 red peppers, cored
   and diced

2 cups chopped broccoli

1 cup chopped cashews

1 cup crumbled
   feta cheese

½ cup red wine vinegar

½ cup extra-virgin
   olive oil

This is an easy pasta salad to throw together for a last-minute potluck picnic or meal. It has a little bit of everything, from veggies to nuts to cheese. Don't feel you have to be limited to just what's listed in this recipe; add cauliflower, carrots, and/or olives for even more flavor.

1. Cook the pasta in boiling, salted water until al dente, according to the package directions. Drain the pasta and rinse thoroughly with cool water.

2. In a large mixing bowl, combine the red peppers, broccoli, cashews, and feta cheese. Toss to combine.

3. Add the cooked pasta, tossing to combine.

4. Pour the vinegar and olive oil over the salad and toss to mix well.

5. Refrigerate until ready to serve.

ONE-POT VEGAN MAC AND CHEESE

PREP TIME: 5 MINUTES   **COOK TIME: 20 MINUTES**

DAIRY-FREE, NUT-FREE, OFF THE SHELF, ONE POT, QUICK, VEGAN

SERVES 4

12 ounces uncooked
   macaroni noodles

4 cups oat or rice milk

1 tablespoon cornstarch

2 teaspoons apple
   cider vinegar

1 tablespoon
   Dijon mustard

¾ cup nutritional yeast

1 teaspoon
   onion powder

1 teaspoon garlic powder

Salt

Freshly ground
   black pepper

VARIATION TIP: *Up your
game by giving this a crispy
topping. Before serving,
throw this mac and cheese
in a casserole dish and top
with bread crumbs. Bake
in the oven at 350°F for
5 minutes until the bread
crumbs are golden brown.*

The best vegan mac and cheese I've ever had in my life
comes from a vegan restaurant called Dharma Fine
Vittles in Orlando. It's creamy and hearty and just oh
so good. I have eaten more than my share of mac and
cheese in my attempts at making a vegan cheese sauce,
but love the version I arrived upon because it's light
and tangy.

1. Cook the pasta in boiling, salted water until al dente,
    according to package directions. Drain the pasta and
    set it aside.

2. In the pasta pot, combine the milk, cornstarch, vine-
    gar, mustard, nutritional yeast, onion powder, garlic
    powder, and salt and pepper to taste, and heat over
    medium-high heat. Let it cook for about 5 minutes,
    until the sauce begins to thicken.

3. Add the pasta back to the pot, and stir to combine
    well. Serve immediately.

PIEROGIS AND TOMATOES

PREP TIME: **5 MINUTES**   COOK TIME: **20 MINUTES**

5-INGREDIENT, NUT-FREE, ONE POT, QUICK

SERVES 4

1 tablespoon olive oil

1 garlic clove, minced

1 (28-ounce) can diced tomatoes, drained

¼ cup chopped fresh flat leaf parsley

1 (12-count) package potato-stuffed pierogis, thawed

VARIATION TIP: *Add broccoli and carrots to add color, texture, and flavor. Substitute the canned tomatoes for the broiled cherry tomatoes from the tip in the recipe for Avocado and Lemon Pasta (page 88).*

Pierogis are dough dumplings (similar to ravioli), traditionally stuffed with potatoes or sauerkraut and originally eaten in Central and Eastern Europe. These days, they're stuffed with anything from potatoes to fruit purees. They're also readily available in the freezer case at your local grocery store. They make a hearty, all-in-one meal and are super quick to fix.

1. In a large saucepan, heat the oil over medium-high heat. Add the garlic and stir for 2 minutes, until fragrant. Add the canned tomatoes and chopped parsley, and simmer for 5 minutes.

2. Add the perogis to the saucepan, and gently stir to coat with the tomatoes. Let the dish simmer for about 10 minutes, until the perogis are heated through. Serve immediately.

PEANUT SLAW AND RICE NOODLES

DAIRY-FREE, QUICK

SERVES 4

6 cups water

1 (9-ounce) package Japanese buckwheat soba noodles

¾ cup peanut butter

½ cup very hot water, plus more as needed

2 tablespoons soy sauce

Juice of 2 limes

1 tablespoon honey

1 cup shredded coleslaw mix

¾ cup chopped peanuts

2 tablespoons chopped scallions, green parts only

4 lime wedges, for serving

I could literally eat peanut sauce on everything, from noodles to veggies to directly in my mouth. This is a simple, no-fuss peanut sauce that will find its way frequently into your weekly meal rotation. I like to save time and buy pre-shredded coleslaw mix, but if you prefer, you can shred the cabbage and carrots separately.

1. Bring the water to a rapid boil over the stove. Add the noodles and cook for 4 minutes, then drain.

2. While the noodles are cooking, in a medium mixing bowl, whisk together the peanut butter and hot water until the sauce is creamy. Add more water, as needed, 1 tablespoon at a time, to achieve a creamy consistency. Stir in the soy sauce, lime juice, and honey.

3. Transfer the cooked rice noodles to the mixing bowl with the sauce and toss to coat.

4. Divide the rice noodles among 4 plates, and top with coleslaw mix, peanuts, and scallions. Serve immediately with the lime wedges.

MAKE IT VEGAN: Use maple syrup instead of honey to make it vegan. Although most peanut butter is vegan, some major brands are not. Double check the label to make sure.

INGREDIENT TIP: Japanese soba buckwheat noodles are found in the international aisle in the grocery store. You could also substitute with plain spaghetti noodles if you cannot find the soba noodles. If you are buying raw honey, look for honey that is lighter in color, opaque or cream colored, and slightly crystalized. I love buying local sourced honey at my local farmer's market.

EGGPLANT AND GARLIC NOODLES

PREP TIME: **10 MINUTES**   COOK TIME: **20 MINUTES**

5-INGREDIENT, DAIRY-FREE, NUT-FREE, QUICK, VEGAN

SERVES 4

2 medium eggplants, peeled and cut into 1-inch cubes

Salt

Freshly ground black pepper

Olive oil spray

12 ounces thin spaghetti noodles

2 tablespoons olive oil

2 garlic cloves, minced

2 tablespoons chopped scallions, green parts, for garnishing

There is a lot of debate on whether to salt eggplant before cooking. New varieties of eggplant don't require salting, and smaller eggplants are less bitter. However, if you do choose to salt yours, put the cubed eggplant in a colander and sprinkle it with salt. Let it sit for one hour, then be sure to rinse off the salt and pat the eggplant dry before baking.

1. Preheat the oven to 400°F. Line a large baking sheet with parchment paper.

2. Spread the eggplant cubes in a single layer on the baking sheet, sprinkle with salt and pepper to taste, and very lightly spray with olive oil. Bake the eggplant for 20 minutes, stirring halfway through, until it is slightly browned.

3. While the eggplant is baking, cook the pasta in boiling, salted water until al dente, according to package directions.

4. Drain the pasta. Then, in the empty pasta pot, heat the oil over medium-high heat. Add the garlic, stirring until fragrant, about 2 minutes. Add the pasta, and stir to coat with the garlic and olive oil.

5. When the eggplant has finished cooking, add the cubed eggplant to the pasta and stir to blend. Divide the pasta among the serving dishes, and garnish with chopped scallions. Serve immediately.

Chocolate-Berry Cobbler, page 104

Sweet Treats

◇

CHOCOLATE-BERRY COBBLER

PREP TIME: **5 MINUTES**   COOK TIME: **35 TO 40 MINUTES**

OFF THE SHELF

SERVES 6

Olive oil spray

1 (15-ounce) box choc-
olate muffin mix,
plus the ingredients
required on the box

3 cups frozen
mixed berries

2 tablespoons granu-
lated sugar

1 tablespoon lemon juice

Confectioners' sugar,
for serving

What is better than a berry cobbler? How about a *chocolate*
berry cobbler? That's right, this warm, fruity treat takes
it to the next level by adding chocolate. Make it easy for
yourself by using a box of chocolate muffin mix to start.
The only thing that would make this dish more of a dream
is a giant scoop of vanilla ice cream melting over the top.
Maybe a drizzle of chocolate syrup, some whipped cream,
a cherry . . . I digress.

1. Preheat the oven to 350°F. Spray a 9-inch round
   baking dish with olive oil spray.

2. In a large mixing bowl, prepare the muffin mix according to the package directions. Do not bake them yet;
   just set the mixture aside.

3. In a saucepan, combine the berries, granulated sugar,
   and lemon juice, and heat over medium heat. Bring to
   a boil, then reduce heat to a simmer. Let it simmer for
   10 minutes, until the berries begin to burst.

4. Pour the berry compote in the bottom of the baking
   dish. Dollop the chocolate muffin batter over the
   berries in sections.

5. Bake for 25 to 30 minutes, until the muffin batter
   is puffed and dry, careful not to let the muffin
   batter burn.

6. Dust with confectioners' sugar before serving.

MANGO-BANANA WHIP

PREP TIME: 5 MINUTES

GLUTEN-FREE, NO COOK, ONE POT, QUICK, VEGAN

SERVES 4

1½ cups vanilla nondairy creamer

1½ cups vanilla almond milk

2 bananas

2 (16-ounce) packages frozen mango chunks

VARIATION TIP: *Replace the mango with pineapple for a nice tropical varia-tion. Top this with toasted coconut flakes or chopped toasted nuts for a bit of extra texture and flavor.*

I love desserts I can whip up in a flash and enjoy right away. This treat is reminiscent of ice cream, but most of the sweetness comes from fruit. It's the prefect hot weather treat, and reminds me of a treat a certain theme park is known for.

1. In a food processor, combine the creamer, almond milk, bananas, and mango chunks. Process up to 5 minutes, until the mixture is a smooth consistency.

2. Divide among serving dishes and serve immediately.

STRAWBERRY-LEMONADE ICE POPS

PREP TIME: **5 MINUTES, PLUS 12 HOURS FREEZING**
COOK TIME: **15 MINUTES**

5-INGREDIENT, DAIRY-FREE, GLUTEN-FREE, NUT-FREE, VEGAN

MAKES 12 ICE POPS

1 (16-ounce) package
  frozen strawberries

¼ cup white sugar

1 tablespoon lemon juice

¼ teaspoon salt

3 cups lemonade

VARIATION TIP: *Replace the strawberries with frozen blueberries, peaches, or a bag of mixed berries. Replace the lemonade with chocolate milk for a chocolate-strawberry version. You get the added benefit of protein and calcium.*

Don't run for that neighborhood ice-cream truck anymore. It's super easy and fun to make your own ice pops at home. You can control the amount of sugar, and the varieties are endless. I love strawberries with lemon, but peaches and cherries make great summer treats as well. Ice-pop molds and sticks are easy to find in your grocery store or online. Silicone molds work best because they won't stick to the ice pops.

1. In a saucepan, combine the strawberries, sugar, lemon juice, and salt, and bring to a boil. Let it simmer for 15 minutes. Pour the strawberry mixture into a blender and blend until pureed; leave the lid of the blender slightly ajar and wrap it in a kitchen towel so the bowl doesn't break. Let the mixture cool completely, about 15 minutes.

2. Pour the strawberry puree into an ice-pop mold, filling each cavity up about one-third full. Top the strawberry with the lemonade, and add the stick. Put the ice pops in the freezer and freeze overnight.

PUFF-PASTRY SOPAPILLAS

PREP TIME: **10 MINUTES**   COOK TIME: **15 MINUTES**

5-INGREDIENT, DAIRY-FREE, NUT-FREE, QUICK

SERVES 6

Olive oil spray

1 cup sugar

1 tablespoon ground
cinnamon

1 sheet puff
pastry, thawed

½ cup honey

I spent just about every Friday night of my childhood in a Mexican restaurant eating sopapillas, a type of light and airy fritter tossed in cinnamon and sugar. This version is a lot better for you because traditional sopapillas are deep-fried, not baked. Plus, this recipe cheats a bit, using prepared puff pastry in lieu of making the pastry from scratch. But think of it this way: Not making the pastry from scratch leaves you with so much more time to enjoy eating them instead.

1. Preheat the oven to 400°F. Line a large baking sheet with parchment paper, and spray it lightly with olive oil spray.

2. In a medium mixing bowl, combine the sugar and cinnamon.

3. Place the sheet of puff pastry on a clean work surface. Cut it into 2-inch squares and place them onto the prepared baking sheet (you may have to work in batches).

4. Bake the puff pastry for 15 minutes, until golden brown. While the puff pastries are still hot, carefully toss them in with the sugar-cinnamon mixture, and then place them on the serving plate.

5. Drizzle with honey and serve hot.

CHOCOLATE HUMMUS

PREP TIME: **5 MINUTES**

5-INGREDIENT, NO COOK, ONE POT, QUICK, VEGAN

SERVES 6

1 (15-ounce) can
chickpeas, drained
and rinsed

¼ cup tahini

¼ cup pure maple syrup

½ cup unsweetened
cocoa powder

¼ teaspoon salt

1 teaspoon
vanilla extract

VARIATION TIP: *Add
chopped nuts or chocolate
chips for some texture.*

Hummus isn't just for snack time anymore. Yes, that's right. Hummus makes a yummy dessert, perfect for dipping strawberries, graham crackers, pound cake, marshmallows, or simply eating by the spoonful. No one ever thinks of dessert as a time to get an infusion of nutrients. But, with this chocolate hummus, you will get an intake of protein, fiber, and calcium. Who knew dessert could be so good for you?

In a food processor, combine the chickpeas, tahini, maple syrup, cocoa powder, salt, and vanilla, and process until smooth. Serve immediately or store in an airtight container in the refrigerator for up to 1 week.

APPLE-PIE DUMP CAKE

PREP TIME: 10 MINUTES   **COOK TIME: 30 MINUTES**

OFF THE SHELF

SERVES 6 TO 8

Olive oil spray

1 (15.25-ounce) box
vanilla cake mix,
plus the ingredients
required on the box

1 (20-ounce) can
apple-pie filling

½ cup chopped pecans

¼ cup unsalted
butter, melted

Whipped cream
(optional)

A dump cake is one of the easiest and tastiest desserts to make. It's basically a hybrid cake/cobbler where you dump all the ingredients into a baking dish and bake, no mixing necessary. A dump cake is versatile, as the name implies. Here, you can swap out the apple pie filling for cherry- or blueberry-pie filling. The pecans and butter are not absolutely necessary, but both add another layer of texture that makes this dessert spectacular.

1. Preheat the oven to 350°F. Spray a 9-by-13-inch glass baking dish with olive oil spray.

2. In a large mixing bowl, prepare the cake mix according to the package directions. Do not bake it yet; just set the mixture aside.

3. Pour the apple-pie filling into the bottom of the pre-pared baking dish. Pour the cake mix on top. Sprinkle the top of the cake with the pecans and drizzle it with the butter. Bake for 30 minutes, until the cake is golden brown. Serve warm, topped with whipped cream, if desired.

NO-BAKE BROWNIE BITES

PREP TIME: **10 MINUTES, PLUS 30 MINUTES CHILLING IN THE REFRIGERATOR**

GLUTEN-FREE, NO COOK, OFF THE SHELF

SERVES 6 TO 8

½ cup almond butter

¼ cup pure maple syrup

¼ cup unsweetened cocoa powder

1 teaspoon pure vanilla extract

⅓ cup gluten-free rolled oats

½ cup milk chocolate chips

½ cup chopped walnuts (optional)

VARIATION TIPS: *Anything you can add to a brownie, you can add here. Use butterscotch or toffee chips instead of the chocolate chips; use pecans instead of the walnuts. Add sweetened coconut flakes or colorful sprinkles.*

MAKE IT VEGAN: *Use dairy-free chocolate chips in place of the milk chocolate chips.*

So easy. So delicious. So popular. When I make these, I make two batches and hide one for myself. This can be our little secret, but these brownies double as protein/health bars because between the oats and almond butter, you're enjoying protein, fiber, antioxidants, and many other essential vitamins.

1. Line a baking sheet with parchment paper. In a large mixing bowl, combine the almond butter, syrup, cocoa powder, vanilla, oats, chocolate chips, and walnuts, if using. Mix well.

2. Using your hands, roll the mixture into ping-pong-size balls, and put them on the prepared baking sheet. Chill them in the refrigerator for 30 minutes, until firm. Store them in the refrigerator in an airtight container for up to week, if they last that long.

CHOCOLATE-BEET BROWNIES

PREP TIME: **10 MINUTES**   COOK TIME: **30 TO 35 MINUTES**

NUT-FREE, OFF THE SHELF

SERVES 6 TO 8

Cooking spray

1 (7-ounce) dark choco-
late bar with at least
80% cocoa, chopped

1 tablespoon
unsalted butter

1 (14.5-ounce) can
beets, drained

3 large eggs

1 teaspoon
vanilla extract

1 cup light brown sugar

2 tablespoons unsweet-
ened cocoa powder

1 teaspoon
baking powder

This is one of my signature (and namesake) recipes from my website, *Beauty and the Beets*. I have had even the most skeptical non-beet-eaters tell me they can't tell there are beets in this recipe. It just goes to show that you can hide vegetables in desserts, and your veggie-haters will never know. But why would you hide beets in your brownies? Because beets are full of fiber, iron, and vitamin C.

1. Preheat the oven to 400°F. Spray a 9-by-13-inch baking pan with cooking spray.

2. In a glass measuring cup, combine the chopped chocolate and butter, and heat in the microwave in 10-second increments, stirring between intervals, until the chocolate is fully melted.

3. In a food processor, puree the beets until smooth. Add the melted chocolate and butter, eggs, and vanilla. Pulse until smooth. Add the brown sugar, cocoa powder, and baking powder, and pulse until the batter is smooth.

4. Pour the batter into the baking pan, and bake for 30 to 35 minutes. The brownies are done when they begin to pull away from the side of the pan and a toothpick inserted into the brownies comes out with just a few fudgy crumbs attached.

BANANA-BREAD COOKIES

PREP TIME: **10 MINUTES**   COOK TIME: **20 MINUTES**

5-INGREDIENT, GLUTEN-FREE, QUICK

SERVES 8

3 ripe bananas

1 large egg,
  lightly beaten

1 cup almond flour

3 tablespoons pure
  maple syrup

½ teaspoon
  vanilla extract

¼ cup chocolate chips
  (optional)

VARIATION TIP: *Add ¼ to
½ cup rolled oats to turn
these from dessert cookies
into breakfast cookies that
would pass any parent's
test. Add nuts to step 2 for
more protein and crunch.*

Banana bread is the most common and delicious way to use overripe bananas. Let's try something a little bit different here. These cookies have the same mouthwatering taste, but they are completely portable. Pack in lunches, pop in your mouth as a quick, not-that-bad-for-you sweet treat, or bring them to a potluck. Keep in mind that the riper your bananas, the more intense the banana flavor will be.

1. Preheat the oven to 350°F. Line a baking sheet with parchment paper.

2. In a food processor, combine the bananas, beaten egg, flour, maple syrup, vanilla, and chocolate chips, if using. Pulse until it forms a smooth batter.

3. In 2-tablespoon increments, dollop the dough onto the baking sheet, about 1 inch apart.

4. Bake for about 20 minutes, until the cookies are golden brown.

5. Transfer the cookies to a cooling rack, and let them cool before serving or storing. Store in an airtight container for up to 5 days.

SPEEDY CANNOLI DIP

PREP TIME: **5 MINUTES, PLUS 10 MINUTES CHILLING IN THE REFRIGERATOR**

GLUTEN-FREE, NO COOK, NUT-FREE, ONE POT, QUICK

SERVES 4 TO 6

1 cup ricotta cheese

½ cup cream cheese

¾ cup confection-
ers' sugar

½ teaspoon
vanilla extract

¼ teaspoon ground
cinnamon

¾ cup miniature semi-
sweet chocolate chips

Cannoli were reportedly popularized by Sicilians (some say their Arab ancestors actually created the dessert), as a treat for a carnival and were said to symbolize fertility. Just like the Chocolate Hummus (page 108), this cannoli dip is easy to throw together, requires very little chill time, and is difficult to stop eating. Serve with fresh strawberries or broken waffle cone pieces for a taste of Sicily in just 15 minutes.

1. In a food processor, combine the ricotta cheese, cream cheese, confectioners' sugar, vanilla, and cinnamon. Pulse until well blended.

2. Fold in the chocolate chips, then chill for 10 minutes in the refrigerator before serving.

Measurement Conversions

VOLUME EQUIVALENTS	U.S. STANDARD	U.S. STANDARD (OUNCES)	METRIC (APPROXIMATE)
LIQUID	2 tablespoons	1 fl. oz.	30 mL
	¼ cup	2 fl. oz.	60 mL
	½ cup	4 fl. oz.	120 mL
	1 cup	8 fl. oz.	240 mL
	1½ cups	12 fl. oz.	355 mL
	2 cups or 1 pint	16 fl. oz.	475 mL
	4 cups or 1 quart	32 fl. oz.	1 L
	1 gallon	128 fl. oz.	4 L
DRY	⅛ teaspoon	–	0.5 mL
	¼ teaspoon	–	1 mL
	½ teaspoon	–	2 mL
	¾ teaspoon	–	4 mL
	1 teaspoon	–	5 mL
	1 tablespoon	–	15 mL
	¼ cup	–	59 mL
	⅓ cup	–	79 mL
	½ cup	–	118 mL
	⅔ cup	–	156 mL
	¾ cup	–	177 mL
	1 cup	–	235 mL
	2 cups or 1 pint	–	475 mL
	3 cups	–	700 mL
	4 cups or 1 quart	–	1 L
	½ gallon	–	2 L
	1 gallon	–	4 L

OVEN TEMPERATURES

FAHRENHEIT	CELSIUS (APPROXIMATE)
250°F	120°C
300°F	150°C
325°F	165°C
350°F	180°C
375°F	190°C
400°F	200°C
425°F	220°C
450°F	230°C

WEIGHT EQUIVALENTS

U.S. STANDARD	METRIC (APPROXIMATE)
½ ounce	15 g
1 ounce	30 g
2 ounces	60 g
4 ounces	115 g
8 ounces	225 g
12 ounces	340 g
16 ounces or 1 pound	455 g

Index

O

Acknowledgments

To Chad, without you, none of this would be possible. Thank you for celebrating my accomplishments and never letting me give up when I fail. Thank you for having an open palate and an open mind. I promise you I will always leave the mushrooms out for you. To John and Chris—for eating my raw cookie dough every day after school. It was the beginning of my recipe-developing skills, and thankfully, I moved on to healthier and tastier foods since. Thank you to my mom, who is always up for a food discussion, and will spend days running around New York City in search of the perfect grilled cheese sandwich. To Steve, who won't eat Brussels sprouts, stop telling the kids they are so yucky or they won't grow up big and strong. To Eva, Mae, and Grey—eat your Brussels sprouts so you grow up big and strong. Thank you to Dad and Sharon, who still probably haven't thrown out that bowl of Jell-O I made when I was 12. It never jiggled, and if it hasn't jiggled by now, you can probably go ahead and toss it. I think we can all agree that Jell-O isn't one of my specialties. To Amy Barrie, who tried to teach me how to cook after college. Thank you for never letting me go hungry even when I couldn't find the vacuum cleaner to earn my keep. To Ashley, Cecily, Caryn, and everyone else at Callisto for finding me, believing in me, and working with me to get this book written and published.

About the Author

Anna-Marie Walsh is a food and travel writer currently based in Orlando, Florida. She has been the founder and content creator behind the food and travel website Beauty and the Beets for the last 10 years. Anna-Marie holds a journalism degree from Arizona State University and in her past lives was a dancer at Walt Disney World, a Muppet puppeteer, and a flight attendant with Delta Airlines. When she is not in the kitchen cooking or at a desk writing, she runs half marathons, golfs, and spends time with her fur children, Charlotte, Olive, and Finnegan.

CPSIA information can be obtained
at www.ICGtesting.com
Printed in the USA
BVHW021529161021
619025BV00005B/6